NEW EDITION

Practice Tests

IELTS

Plus 3 with Key

Margaret Matthews
Katy Salisbury

TEACHING NOT JUST TESTING

PEARSON
Longman

Pearson Education Limited
Edinburgh Gate
Harlow
Essex CM20 2JE
England
and Associated Companies throughout the world.

www.longman.com

First published 2011

ISBN: 978-1-4082-6790-5
Book with key and Multi-ROM and Audio CD pack

ISBN: 978-1-4082-6252-8
Book with key for pack

ISBN: 978-1-4082-6253-5
Multi-ROM for pack

ISBN: 978-1-4082-8034-8
Audio CD for pack

Set in 10.5pt Arial Regular
Printed in Slovakia by Neografia

Acknowledgements

For Hannah and George

The authors would like to thank the following people: Jonathan Salisbury and the students of Mayflower College, Plymouth and the students of Bell (www.bell-centres.com) and International House, London for their valuable help in trialling writing and speaking papers; Rosemary Coop for her hard work producing detailed answer keys and offering general advice; Malcolm Fletcher for his helpful comments on reading tasks.

We are grateful to the following for permission to reproduce copyright material:

Figures
Figure on page 73 "Graduate joblessness by gender 2008 to 2009", copyright © ONS, Crown Copyright material is reproduced with the permission of the Controller, Office of Public Sector Information (OPSI); and Figure on page 111 from *The Management of Weeds in Irrigation and Drainage Channels*, Water, Engineering and Development Centre (Smout, I.K., Wade, P.M., Baker, P.J. and Ferguson, C.M.) p.36, http://www.dfid-kar-water.net/w5outputs/electronic_outputs/management_of_weeds.pdf, copyright © WEDC, Loughborough University, 1997.

Text
Interview on page 14 adapted from "Juniper – down the hatch?", 28 April 2010, www.plantlife.org.uk, copyright © Plantlife; Extract on pages 16-17 adapted from "Case study Isle of Eigg Heritage Trust, Scotland" The Ashden Awards, accessed on 20.07.10, pp.1-3, copyright © The Ashden Awards for Sustainable Energy, www.ashdenawards.org; Extract on pages 20-21 from *The Context of Organizational Change*, Prentice Hall & FT (Senior, B. and Fleming, J. 2006) pp.7-15, copyright © Pearson Education Ltd; Extract on pages 24-25 adapted from *Memory and Emotion*, Weidenfeld and Nicolson (McGaugh, J. 2003) pp.40-44, copyright © Weidenfeld and Nicolson, an imprint of The Orion Publishing Group, London; Extract on page 45 adapted from *How Bad Are Bananas?*, Profile Books (Berners-Lee, M. 2010) pp.146-148, copyright © Profile Books; Extract on pages 47-48 adapted from "The Pottery-Producing System at Akrotiri: An index of Exchange and Social Activity", *The Thera Foundation* (L. Katsa-Tomara), copyright © Litsa Katsa-Tomara; Extract on pages 61-62 adapted from *Hope for Animals and Their World*, Icon Books (Jane Goodall with Thane Maynard and Gail Hudson 2010) pp.19-22, copyright © 2009. Reproduced courtesy of Icon Books, London, UK; Extract on pages 69-70 adapted from "A reputation in tatters", *New Scientist*, 29/05/2010, pp.26-27 (Ward, B.), copyright © New Scientist Magazine; Extract on pages 81-82 adapted from "Music retailer – a new-tech pioneer", *Brisbane Times*, pp.1-2 (Rod Myer, 2010), copyright © Rod Myer, a Melbourne writer and journalist; Extract on pages 86-87 adapted from *Thames: Sacred River*, Chatto and Windus (Peter Ackroyd, 2007) pp.162-165. Copyright © Peter Ackroyd 2007. Reproduced with permission of The Random House Group and Sheil Land Associates Ltd; Extract on pages 89-90 adapted from "Diminutive Subjects, Design Strategy, and Driving Sales: Preschoolers and the Nintendo DS" by J. Alison Bryant, Anna Akerman, Jordana Drell, http://gamestudies.org. Reproduced by permission of Dr Alison Bryant; Interview on page 99 adapted from *Bird Table*, Winter 2009, BTO (Mike Toms, 2009) pp.15-17, copyright © The British Trust for Ornithology; Extract on pages 100-101 adapted from *Poverty and Reefs Vol 1 A Global Review*, DFID / IMM Ltd (Whittingham, E., Campbell, J. and Townsley, P.) pp.3 & 31-34, copyright © 2003 IMM Ltd, Exeter, UK; Extract on pages 104-105 adapted from *Cognitive and Language Development in Children*, Open University (Oates, J. and Grayson, A. 2004) pp.288-293. Reproduced by permission of The Open University; Extract on pages 107-108 from *Learning from the past*, Penguin Books (J. Diamond, 2005) pp.5-15, copyright © Jared Diamond, 2005. Reproduced with permission from Jared Diamond and Penguin Books Ltd; Interview on pages 114-115 adapted from "Cut costs and time, not corners", *The Observer Magazine*, 20/06/2010, p.32 (Dulux Advertisement Feature), reproduced with permission of Dulux, ICI Paints; Extract on pages 126-127 from "Talking Heads", *New Scientist*, 29/05/2010, pp.33-35 (Kenneally, C.), copyright © New Scientist Magazine; Interview on page 137 adapted from 2009 Ashden Awards Case Study by Vincent Stauffer, copyright © The Ashden Awards for Sustainable Energy, www.ashdenawards.org; Extract on pages 142-143 adapted from "A cave man blinking in the light", *The Economist*, 08/05/2010, pp.83-84, copyright © The Economist 2010; Extract on pages 146-147 from *The Unnatural History of the Sea*, Gaia (Callum Roberts, 2007) pp.374-376, copyright © 2007 Callum, M. Roberts. Reproduced by permission of Island Press, Washington, DC; Extract on page 156 adapted from 'Volunteer Signup', MNDNR, http://www.dnr.state.mn.us/volunteering/signup.html, copyright © 2010, State of Minnesota, Department of Natural Resources. Reprinted with permission; Extract on pages 158-159 adapted from "Seven Top Tips on How to get up the Career Ladder", *Personnel Today* (Accessed on 27.08.10), www.personneltoday.com, copyright © Personnel Today Group; and Extract on pages 161-162 adapted from *Bird Table*, Summer 2009, Issue 58, BTO (Mike Toms 2009) pp.14-17, copyright © The British Trust for Ornithology.

Every effort has been made to trace the copyright holders and we apologise in advance for any unintentional omissions. We would be pleased to insert the appropriate acknowledgement in any subsequent edition of this publication.

CONTENTS

INTRODUCTION TO IELTS

IELTS stands for *International English Language Testing System.* It is a test of English language skills designed for students who want to study in the medium of English either at university, college or secondary school.

There are two versions of the test: the **Academic Module** and the **General Training (GT) Module**. Students wishing to study at postgraduate or undergraduate levels should take the Academic Module. The General Training Module is designed for those candidates who plan to undertake training or secondary school education. The General Training Module is also used in Australia, Canada, New Zealand and the UK to assess the language skills of incoming migrants. Candidates must decide in advance which of the two modules they wish to sit as the results are not interchangeable.

Students sit the Listening, Reading and Writing papers in that order on one day. The Speaking Test may be held up to two days later, though normally it is taken on the same day, after the Writing Test.

A computerised version of the Listening, Reading and Writing Tests is available at many IELTS centres, but the paper-based version of IELTS will always be offered and is the standard format.

Overview of the test

The test is in four parts reflecting the four basic language skills:

- **Listening:** *taken by all candidates*
- **Reading:** *Academic or General Training*
- **Writing:** *Academic or General Training*
- **Speaking:** *taken by all candidates*

Results

Performance is rated on a scale of 0–9. Candidates receive a Test Report Form, which shows their overall performance reported as a single band score as well as the individual scores they received for each part of the test.

The IELTS nine-band scale

Band 9 – Expert user
Has fully operational command of the language: appropriate, accurate and fluent with complete understanding.

Band 8 – Very good user
Has fully operational command of the language with only occasional unsystematic inaccuracies and inappropriacies. Misunderstandings may occur in unfamiliar situations. Handles complex detailed argumentation well.

Band 7 – Good user
Has operational command of the language, though with occasional inaccuracies, inappropriacies and misunderstandings in some situations. Generally handles complex language well and understands detailed reasoning.

Band 6 – Competent user
Has generally effective command of the language despite some inaccuracies, inappropriacies and misunderstandings. Can use and understand fairly complex language, particularly in familiar situations.

Band 5 – Modest user
Has partial command of the language, coping with overall meaning in most situations, though is likely to make many mistakes. Should be able to handle basic communication in own field.

Band 4 – Limited user
Basic competence is limited to familiar situations. Has frequent problems in understanding and expression. Is not able to use complex language.

Band 3 – Extremely limited user
Conveys and understands only general meaning in very familiar situations. Frequent breakdowns in communication occur.

Band 2 – Intermittent user
No real communication is possible except for the most basic information using isolated words or short formulas in familiar situations and to meet immediate needs. Has great difficulty in understanding spoken and written English.

Band 1 – Non user
Essentially has no ability to use the language beyond possibly a few isolated words.

Band 0 – Did not attempt the test
No assessable information provided.

Overview of the IELTS Test

Listening (played once only; approx 30 minutes + 10 minutes transfer time)

	No. of items	Discourse types	No. of speakers	Task types	Target listening skills
Section 1	10	A transactional conversation – general context.	2	• multiple choice • short answer questions	• listening for main ideas • listening for specific information
Section 2	10	An informational talk – general context.	1	• notes/table/form/flow chart/sentence completion	
Section 3	10	A conversation – education/training context.	2–4	• summary completion • plan/map/diagram labelling	• understanding speaker's opinion
Section 4	10	A lecture – education/training context.	1	• matching • classification	
Overall	40			Up to 3 task types per passage	

Academic Reading (60 minutes)

	No. of items	Text types	Task types	Target reading skills
Passage 1	13–14	Academic texts, i.e. journals, newspapers, textbooks and magazines. Generally accessible rather than discipline-specific. Graded in difficulty.	• multiple choice • short answer questions • notes/table/form/flow chart/sentence/summary completion • diagram labelling • matching paragraph headings • matching lists/sentence endings • locating information in paragraphs • True/False/Not Given • Yes/No/Not Given	• skimming and scanning • understanding main ideas • reading for detail • understanding opinion and attitude
Passage 2	13–14			
Passage 3	13–14			
Overall	40	Total of 2,000–2,750 words	Up to 4 task types per passage	

Academic Writing (60 minutes)

	No. of tasks	Text types	Task types	Target writing skills
Task 1 (20 mins) Carries one-third of marks	1	A summarising description of graphic or pictorial input.	Information transfer exercise. (No explanations of the information required.)	• present, describe, interpret, compare quantitative data • describe a process or how something works
Task 2 (40 mins) Carries two-thirds of marks	1	An extended piece of discursive writing.	Candidates are presented with a given point of view or problem on which to base an organised, extended response.	• argue, defend or attack a point of view using supporting evidence • identify causes and/or suggest a solution to a problem • compare and contrast opinions • evaluate the effects of a development
Overall	2	Minimum of 150 words (Task 1) Minimum of 250 words (Task 2)		Task requirements selected from the range above

General Training Reading (60 minutes)

	No. of items	Text types	Task types	Target reading skills
Section 1 Social survival	13–14	Informational texts related to everyday situations.	• multiple choice • short answer questions • notes/table/form/flow chart/sentence/summary completion • diagram labelling • matching lists/sentence endings • matching paragraph headings • True/False/Not Given • locating information in paragraphs	• skimming and scanning • understanding main ideas • reading for detail • understanding opinion and attitude
Section 2 Work related	13–14	Texts from a work place/ training context but related to the survival needs of students.		
Section 3 General reading	13–14	One descriptive or narrative text on a topic of general interest.		
Overall	40	2,000–2,750 words	Up to 4 task types per passage	

General Training Writing (60 minutes)

	No. of tasks	Text types	Task types	Target writing skills
Task 1 (20 mins) Carries one-third of marks	1	A short letter – informal, semi-formal or formal style.	An input prompt poses a problem or describes a situation which requires a written response in letter format. Three bullet points outline what should be included in the letter.	• respond to task • use letter writing style • include the information highlighted in the bullets
Task 2 (40 mins) Carries two-thirds of marks	1	An extended piece of discursive writing.	An extended, organised response to questions or issues raised in the task.	• express and justify a point of view on the topic • compare and contrast opinions drawing on personal experience • evaluation a situation or development • consider the causes of a problem and suggest possible solutions
Overall	2	Minimum of 150 words (Task 1) Minimum of 250 words (Task 2)		Task requirements selected from the range above

Speaking (11–14 minutes)

	No. of parts	Format: Individual interview with an examiner	Nature of interaction	Target speaking skills
Part 1	4–5 minutes	Introduction and interview.	Examiner asks set questions about familiar topics, using a fixed framework.	• giving personal information • talking about everyday issues and habits • expressing opinions
Part 2	3–4 minutes	Individual long turn.	Candidate has to speak for about two minutes on a topic chosen by the examiner. Candidate is given one minute to prepare and can make notes in that time.	• showing an ability to keep going without interlocutor support • managing language: organisation and expression of ideas • using a range of language appropriately
Part 3	4–5 minutes	Exploring the topic – developing a discussion.	Examiner leads the candidate to consider more general issues related to the Part 2 topic. Candidate is encouraged to develop language of a more abstract nature.	• expressing views and opinions • explaining • displaying understanding of the conversational rules of English

TEST 1

Listening module (approx 30 minutes + 10 minutes transfer time)

Guidance

Overview

The Listening test is taken by both Academic and General Training candidates. It lasts for forty minutes (thirty minutes plus ten minutes transfer time) and consists of four sections. There are a total of forty questions: ten in each section.

The recording is only played ONCE. As you listen, you must note down your answers on the question paper. When the recording is finished you will be given ten minutes to transfer your answers to the answer sheet.

Sections 1 and 2 relate to social contexts, testing the listening skills you need for survival in an English-speaking country. Section 1 is a conversation between two speakers, e.g. two people talking about holiday preparations, and Section 2 is a monologue, e.g. a podcast about what you can do at a theme park.

Sections 3 and 4 have a more academic or training context. Section 3 is a conversation between two or more people, e.g. a seminar between a tutor and a student about a work placement, and Section 4 is a monologue, e.g. a lecturer presenting the findings of a research project.

Before each section, you will hear a brief introduction explaining who the speakers are and what the situation is. You will also be given a short time to look through the questions before the recording for that section starts. In sections 1 to 3, there is a short break in the middle giving you time to look at the questions in the second half. There is no break in Section 4.

All answers will occur in the correct form in the recording (so you will not change it), and you will only get a mark if the answer is correctly spelt. You must also follow the instructions regarding the maximum number of words for each answer.

Tasks

A variety of questions are used, chosen from the following types:
- Multiple choice.
- Note/table/summary/flow chart completion.
- Matching.
- Diagram/map/plan labelling.
- True, false, not given.

In some tasks you will have to write words or phrases, and in other tasks you will have to write letters or numbers.

Tip strip
Questions 1–10

• When you read task instructions, always <u>underline</u> how many words are allowed for each answer. Never write more than the maximum stated, though you *can* use *fewer*. In this task, the maximum number of words you can use is two, but many of the answers are just one word.

• Only write down words you hear, in the form you hear them. If you need to change the form of a word to make it fit grammatically, then it's incorrect.

Example
For Section 1 only, you will be given an example and you will hear the first few lines twice. After that you will only hear the recording once.

Question 1
Listen for a phrase which means the same as 'occupation'.

Question 4
You will hear several numbers mentioned. Don't just write down the first number you hear – wait until the woman confirms how many years she has been a member.

Questions 1–10

Questions 1–10

Complete the form below.

Write **NO MORE THAN TWO WORDS OR A NUMBER** *for each answer.*

Health club customer research

Example	*Answer*
Name:	*Selina Thompson*

Occupation: **1** ....

Age group: **2** ....

Type of membership: **3** ....

Length of membership: **4** .... *years*

Why joined: *Recommended by a* **5** ....

Visits to club per month: *Eight (on an average)* ....

Facility used most: **6** ....

Facility not used (If any): *Tennis courts (because reluctant to* **7** .... *)*

Suggestions for improvements: *Have more* **8** ....

Install **9** .... *in the gym.*

Open **10** .... *later at weekends.*

Tip strip

Question 6 and Question 9
Listen to both speakers. Most of the answers are supplied by the woman, but not all of them. For Questions **6** and **9**, the man suggests something and the woman agrees.

Question 8
Be careful with answers which require plural endings. You will not get a mark if you leave off the 's'.

Questions 8–10
There are three suggestions for improvements listed. Carefully read the words given for each bullet point: this will tell you where to note each suggested improvement. You will lose a mark if you do not put the word in the correct gap.

Questions 11–20

Tip strip
Questions 11–16

- As with all flow chart tasks, listen carefully for the words and phrases which signal the beginning of each new stage in the sequence.
- For this type of question, check how many extra options are given: in this case, there is just ONE.
- In these tasks, options are only used once. (In tasks where you can use options more than once, the instructions will clearly state this.)

Questions 11–16

Complete the flow chart below.

*Choose **SIX** answers from the box and write the correct letter, **A–G**, next to questions 11–16.*

A air	**B** ash	**C** earth	**D** grass
E sticks	**F** stones	**G** water	

Making a steam pit

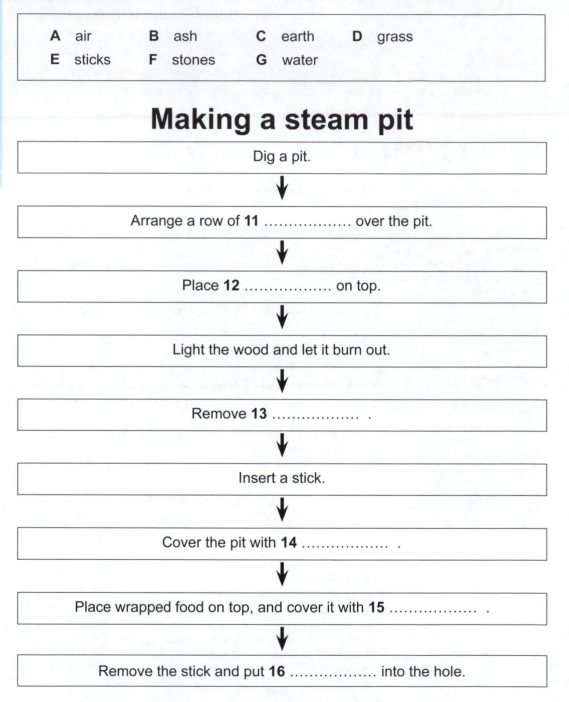

Dig a pit.

↓

Arrange a row of **11** .... over the pit.

↓

Place **12** .... on top.

↓

Light the wood and let it burn out.

↓

Remove **13** ....

↓

Insert a stick.

↓

Cover the pit with **14** ....

↓

Place wrapped food on top, and cover it with **15** ....

↓

Remove the stick and put **16** .... into the hole.

Tip strip
Questions 17–20
- In this type of multiple-choice item, you must choose TWO options from a list of five.
- The options might not be in the same order as the information in the recording.

Questions 17–18

Choose **TWO** letters, **A–E**.

Which **TWO** characteristics apply to the bamboo oven?

- **A** It's suitable for windy weather.
- **B** The fire is lit below the bottom end of the bamboo.
- **C** The bamboo is cut into equal lengths.
- **D** The oven hangs from a stick.
- **E** It cooks food by steaming it.

Questions 19–20

Choose **TWO** letters, **A–E**.

Which **TWO** pieces of advice does the speaker give about eating wild fungi?

- **A** Cooking doesn't make poisonous fungi edible.
- **B** Edible wild fungi can be eaten without cooking.
- **C** Wild fungi are highly nutritious.
- **D** Some edible fungi look very similar to poisonous varieties.
- **E** Fungi which cannot be identified should only be eaten in small quantities.

Questions 21–30

Questions 21–25

*Choose the correct letter, **A**, **B** or **C**.*

Research project on attitudes towards study

21 Phoebe's main reason for choosing her topic was that

   A her classmates had been very interested in it.

   B it would help prepare her for her first teaching post.

   C she had been inspired by a particular book.

22 Phoebe's main research question related to

   A the effect of teacher discipline.

   B the variety of learning activities.

   C levels of pupil confidence.

23 Phoebe was most surprised by her finding that

   A gender did not influence behaviour significantly.

   B girls were more negative about school than boys.

   C boys were more talkative than girls in class.

24 Regarding teaching, Phoebe says she has learned that

   A teachers should be flexible in their lesson planning.

   B brighter children learn from supporting weaker ones.

   C children vary from each other in unpredictable ways.

25 Tony is particularly impressed by Phoebe's ability to

   A recognise the limitations of such small-scale research.

   B reflect on her own research experience in an interesting way.

   C design her research in such a way as to minimise difficulties.

Questions 26–30

What did Phoebe find difficult about the different research techniques she used?

*Choose **FIVE** answers from the box and write the correct letter **A–G**, next to questions 26–30.*

Tip strip
Questions 26–30

- For matching exercises like these, it is important to be clear on the specific task. In this case you must listen for what is DIFFICULT about each of the five research techniques. The focus will also be indicated in the heading of the box: 'Difficulties'.

Difficulties

- **A** Obtaining permission
- **B** Deciding on a suitable focus
- **C** Concentrating while gathering data
- **D** Working collaboratively
- **E** Processing data she had gathered
- **F** Finding a suitable time to conduct the research
- **G** Getting hold of suitable equipment

Research techniques

26 Observing lessons   ....

27 Interviewing teachers   ....

28 Interviewing pupils   ....

29 Using questionnaires   ....

30 Taking photographs   ....

Questions 31–40

Questions 31–40

Complete the sentences below.

*Write **NO MORE THAN TWO WORDS** for each answer.*

Saving the juniper plant

Background

31 Juniper was one of the first plants to colonise Britain after the last
....

32 Its smoke is virtually .... , so juniper wood was used as
fuel in illegal activities.

33 Oils from the plant were used to prevent .... spreading.

34 Nowadays, its berries are widely used to .... food and drink.

Ecology

35 Juniper plants also support several species of insects and ....

Problems

36 In current juniper populations, ratios of the .... are poor.

37 Many of the bushes in each group are of the same age so ....
of whole populations is rapid.

Solutions

38 Plantlife is trialling novel techniques across .... areas of England.

39 One measure is to introduce .... for seedlings.

40 A further step is to plant .... from healthy bushes.

Tip strip

Question 31

Listen for a synonym for 'colonise'.

Question 32

Listen for a synonym for 'illegal'.

Question 37

Listen for a synonym for 'rapid'.

Question 38

Listen for a synonym for 'novel'.

Tip strip

Questions 31–40

- Section 4 of the listening paper is a presentation or lecture. Read the heading and listen carefully to the information given at the beginning of the recording. It tells you who is talking and his/her general subject or field. Also the first part of the lecture itself often gives useful information about the focus.

- The field of this presentation is Environmental Science – knowing this will help you predict what will be important to the speaker: the destruction of an ancient species of plant and ways to protect it.

- Read the sub-headings on the answer sheet. The speaker will clearly state when he/she is changing to a new sub-section. He/She will either mention the word in the heading or give a close paraphrase. Listen for structuring phrases such as 'Turning now to …' or a rhetorical question such as 'Why is the juniper plant declining …?'

Reading module (1 hour)

Guidance

Overview

The Academic Reading test lasts for an hour, and it consists of three parts, so you should spend about twenty minutes on each part. The first part is generally a bit easier than the second and third parts, so you might decide to spend a little less time on this.

As you do the test you can make notes on the question paper, but all your answers have to be written on a separate mark sheet, so you must allow enough time to do this.

The test has a total of 40 questions, so in two of the sections there are 13 questions, and in one there are 14 questions.

Reading passages

The reading passages in all three sections are of a similar length, each one consisting of between 750–950 words. The first passage is usually more factual than the others, and the third contains more opinion. There is a range of topics, and these might be related to any academic subject area, such as natural sciences, history, archaeology or education. However, the subject matter of the passages is not highly technical, and should be accessible to any IELTS candidate, whatever their personal educational history.

Tasks

The Academic Reading paper uses a variety of task types, including:
- Giving short answers to questions.
- Deciding whether statements/opinions correspond to what is written in the reading passage.
- Matching statements to people or events which are mentioned in the reading passage.
- Completing a summary, or individual sentences, which are based on the reading passage.
- Completing a table, a diagram, a flow chart, or notes which are based on the reading passage.
- Choosing a statement about the reading passage from several options.
- Choosing the answer to a question about the reading passage from several options.
- Choosing the best heading for each of the paragraphs in a reading passage.

In some tasks, you will have to write words or phrases, and in other tasks you will have to write letters or numbers.

Reducing electricity consumption on the Isle of Eigg

Background

The Isle of Eigg is situated off the West Coast of Scotland, and is reached by ferry from the mainland. For the island community of about a hundred residents, it has always been expensive to import products, materials and skilled labour from the mainland, and this has encouraged a culture of self-sufficiency and careful use of resources. Today, although the island now has most modern conveniences, CO_2 emissions per household are 20 percent lower than the UK average, and electricity use is 50 percent lower.

When Eigg designed its electricity grid, which was switched on in February 2008, it quickly became apparent that in order to keep the capital building costs down, it would be necessary to manage demand. This would also allow the island to generate most of its electricity from renewable sources, mainly water, wind and solar power. This goal was overseen by the Eigg Heritage Trust (EHT).

The technology

Eigg manages electricity demand mainly by capping the instantaneous power that can be used to five kilowatts (kW) for a household and ten kW for a business. If usage goes over the limit, the electricity supply is cut off and the maintenance team must be called to come and switch it back on again. All households and businesses have energy monitors, which display current and cumulative electricity usage, and sound an alarm when consumption reaches a user-defined level, usually set a few hundred watts below the actual limit. The result is that Eigg residents have a keen sense of how much power different electrical appliances use, and are careful to minimise energy consumption.

Demand is also managed by warning the entire island when renewable energy generation is lower than demand, and diesel generators are operating to back it up – a so-called 'red light day', as opposed to 'green light days' when there is sufficient renewable energy. Residents then take steps to temporarily reduce electricity demand further still, or postpone demand until renewable energy generation has increased.

Energy use on the island has also been reduced through improved wall and loft insulation in homes, new boilers, solar water heating, car-sharing and various small, energy-saving measures in households. New energy supplies are being developed, including sustainably harvested forests to supply wood for heating.

Eigg Heritage Trust has installed insulation in all of its own properties at no cost to the tenants, while private properties have paid for their own insulation to be installed. The same applies for installations of solar water heating, although not all Trust properties have received this as yet. The Trust also operates a Green Grants scheme, where residents can claim 50 percent of the cost of equipment to reduce carbon emissions, up to a limit of £300. Purchases included bikes, solar water heating, secondary glazing, thicker curtains, and greenhouses to grow food locally, rather than importing it.

Environmental benefits

Prior to the installation of the new electricity grid and renewable energy generation, most households on Eigg used diesel generators to supply electricity, resulting in significant carbon emissions. Homes were also poorly insulated and had old, inefficient oil-burning boilers, or used coal for heating.

The work by the Eigg Heritage Trust to reduce energy use has resulted in significant reductions in carbon emissions from the island's households and businesses. The average annual electricity use per household is just 2,160 kilowatt hours (kWh), compared to a UK average in 2008 of 4,198 kWh. Domestic carbon emissions have fallen by 47 percent, from 8.4 to 4.45 tonnes per year. This compares to average UK household emissions of 5.5 to 6 tonnes per year. The emissions should fall even further over the next few years as the supply of wood for heating increases.

Social benefits

The completion of Eigg's electricity grid has made a significant difference to the island's residents, freeing them from dependence on diesel generators and providing them with a stable and affordable power supply. A reliable electricity supply has brought improvements in other areas, for example, better treatment of drinking water in some houses, and the elimination of the constant noise of diesel generators. Improved home insulation and heating has also yielded benefits, making it more affordable to keep homes at a comfortable temperature. One of the incentives for capping electricity use, rather than charging different amounts according to usage, was to make access to energy equitable. Every household has the same five kW cap, irrespective of income, so distributing the available resources equally across the island's population.

Economic and employment benefits

Eigg's electricity grid supports four part-time maintenance jobs on the island, and residents have also been employed for building work to improve Trust-owned houses and other buildings. Likewise, the start of organised harvesting of wood for heating has created several forestry jobs for residents. A part-time 'green project manager' post has also been created. A wider economic impact has come from having a reliable and affordable electricity supply, which has enabled several new businesses to start up, including restaurants, shops, guest houses and self-catering accommodation. As Eigg has become known for cutting carbon emissions and protecting the environment, an increasing number of visitors have come to the island to learn about its work, bringing a further economic benefit to the residents.

Questions 1–7

Tip strip

Questions 1–7

- Only choose words or numbers which appear in the reading passage. *Don't* use your own words.
- *Don't* make any changes to the words from the reading passage. For example, *don't* change a singular noun to a plural noun.
- You *can* use *fewer* words than the maximum number in the instructions.
- *Don't* write *more* words than the instructions tell you.

Question 1

When you're trying to find the answer, look for a word that has a similar meaning to 'approximately'.

Question 3

When you're trying to find the answer, look for a word that has a similar meaning to 'most of'.

Question 7

The answer is a plural noun. Don't leave the plural 's' off the end of the word.

Answer the questions below.

Choose **NO MORE THAN TWO WORDS AND/OR A NUMBER** *from the passage for each answer.*

1 Approximately how many people live on Eigg?

2 What proportion of a UK household's electricity consumption does an Eigg household consume?

3 Apart from wind and sun, where does most of Eigg's electricity come from?

4 What device measures the amount of electricity Eigg's households are using?

5 When renewable energy supplies are insufficient, what backs them up?

6 What has EHT provided free of charge in all the houses it owns?

7 Which gardening aid did some Eigg inhabitants claim grants for?

Do the following statements agree with the information given in Reading Passage 1?

Write

TRUE   *if the statement agrees with the information*
FALSE   *if the statement contradicts the information*
NOT GIVEN *if there is no information on this*

8 Electricity was available for the first time on Eigg when a new grid was switched on.

9 Eigg's carbon emissions are now much lower than before.

10 Wood will soon be the main source of heating on Eigg.

11 Eigg is quieter as a result of having a new electricity supply.

12 Well-off households pay higher prices for the use of extra electricity.

13 The new electricity grid has created additional employment opportunities on Eigg.

Change in business organisations

A The forces that operate to bring about change in organisations can be thought of as winds which are many and varied – from small summer breezes that merely disturb a few papers, to mighty howling gales which cause devastation to structures and operations, causing consequent reorientation of purpose and rebuilding. Sometimes, however, the winds die down to give periods of relative calm, periods of relative organisational stability. Such a period was the agricultural age, which Goodman (1995) maintains prevailed in Europe and western societies as a whole until the early 1700s. During this period, wealth was created in the context of an agriculturally based society influenced mainly by local markets (both customer and labour) and factors outside people's control, such as the weather. During this time, people could fairly well predict the cycle of activities required to maintain life, even if that life might be at little more than subsistence level.

B To maintain the meteorological metaphor, stronger winds of change blew to bring in the Industrial Revolution and the industrial age. Again, according to Goodman, this lasted for a long time, until around 1945. It was characterised by a series of inventions and innovations that reduced the number of people needed to work the land and, in turn, provided the means of production of hitherto rarely obtainable goods; for organisations, supplying these in ever increasing numbers became the aim. To a large extent, demand and supply were predictable, enabling companies to structure their organisations along what Burns and Stalker (1966) described as mechanistic lines, that is as systems of strict hierarchical structures and firm means of control.

C This situation prevailed for some time, with demand still coming mainly from the domestic market and organisations striving to fill the 'supply gap'. Thus the most disturbing environmental influence on organisations of this time was the demand for products, which outstripped supply. The saying attributed to Henry Ford that 'You can have any colour of car so long as it is black', gives a flavour of the supply-led state of the market. Apart from any technical difficulties of producing different colours of car, Ford did not have to worry about customers' colour preferences: he could sell all that he made. Organisations of this period can be regarded as 'task-oriented', with effort being put into increasing production through more effective and efficient production processes.

D As time passed, this favourable period for organisations began to decline. In the neo-industrial age, people became more discriminating in the goods and services they wished to buy and, as technological advancements brought about increased productivity, supply overtook demand. Companies began, increasingly, to look abroad for additional markets.

E At the same time, organisations faced more intensive competition from abroad for their own products and services. In the West, this development was accompanied by a shift in focus from manufacturing to service, whether this merely added value to manufactured products, or whether it was service in its own right. In the neo-industrial age of western countries, the emphasis moved towards adding value to goods and services – what Goodman calls the value-oriented time, as contrasted with the task-oriented and products/services-oriented times of the past.

F Today, in the post-industrial age, most people agree that organisational life is becoming ever more uncertain, as the pace of change quickens and the future becomes less predictable. Writing in 1999, Nadler and Tushman, two US academics, said: 'Poised on the eve of the next century, we are witnessing a profound transformation in the very nature of our business organisations. Historic forces have converged to fundamentally reshape the scope, strategies, and structures of large enterprises.' At a less general level of analysis, Graeme Leach, Chief Economist at the British Institute of Directors, claimed in the Guardian newspaper (2000) that: 'By 2020, the nine-to-five rat race will be extinct and present levels of self-employment, commuting and technology use, as well as age and sex gaps, will have changed beyond recognition.' According to the article, Leach anticipates that: 'In 20 years time, 20-25 percent of the workforce will be temporary workers and many more will be flexible, … 25 percent of people will no longer work in a traditional office and … 50 percent will work from home in some form.' Continuing to use the 'winds of change' metaphor, the expectation is of damaging gale-force winds bringing the need for rebuilding that takes the opportunity to incorporate new ideas and ways of doing things.

G Whether all this will happen is arguable. Forecasting the future is always fraught with difficulties. For instance, Mannermann (1998) sees future studies as part art and part science and notes: 'The future is full of surprises, uncertainty, trends and trend breaks, irrationality and rationality, and it is changing and escaping from our hands as time goes by. It is also the result of actions made by innumerable more or less powerful forces.' What seems certain is that the organisational world is changing at a fast rate – even if the direction of change is not always predictable. Consequently, it is crucial that organisational managers and decision makers are aware of, and able to analyse the factors which trigger organisational change.

Questions 14–18

Tip strip

Questions 14–18

• This information does *not* appear in the same order as it does in the reading passage.

• To find where the answers are, look for words with the same or similar meanings as the words in the questions.

• You may have to read several sentences before you can be sure you have found the appropriate section in the reading passage.

Question 14

The question has 'predictions', so find a paragraph which contains more than one of these.

Question 16

• The word 'warning' does not appear in the reading passage, so you have to look for the same idea expressed in an *indirect* way.

• Find references to future developments which might have negative consequences.

Question 18

To find the answer, look for a phrase with a meaning similar to 'not a high priority', or any references to customers' needs.

*Reading Passage 2 has **SEVEN** paragraphs, A–G.*

Which paragraph contains the following information?

*Write the correct letter, **A–G**.*

14 some specific predictions about businesses and working practices

15 reference to the way company employees were usually managed

16 a warning for business leaders

17 the description of an era notable for the relative absence of change

18 a reason why customer satisfaction was not a high priority

Questions 19–23

Look at the following characteristics (Questions 19–23) and the list of periods below.

*Match each characteristic with the correct period, **A**, **B** or **C**.*

*Write the correct letter, **A**, **B** or **C**.*

NB You may use any letter more than once.

19 a surplus of goods.

20 an emphasis on production quantity.

21 the proximity of consumers to workplaces.

22 a focus on the quality of goods.

23 new products and new ways of working.

List of periods

   A The agricultural age.   **B** The industrial age.

   C The neo-industrial age.

Tip strip

Questions 19–23

• The 'periods' are in the same order as they are in the reading passage.

• Find the relevant paragraphs, then look for words with the same or similar meanings as the words in the questions.

• *Don't* leave any questions unanswered. When you have attempted all the questions, go back and guess any remaining answers.

Question 19

In which age were companies producing more things than they could easily sell?

Question 21

Look for a word which has a meaning connected to 'proximity'.

Question 23

Look for words with a meaning similar to 'new products'.

Complete the summary below.

Choose **ONE WORD ONLY** from the passage for each answer.

Tip strip

Questions 24–26

- You can see from the summary title that it is about the present time, so look for the answers in the last two paragraphs.
- The missing words *may* not be in the same order as they appear in the reading passage.
- *Don't* write more than the number of words you are allowed in the instructions.
- Look only for words which fit the summary grammatically as well as in meaning.
- *Don't* change any words. Write them exactly as they appear in the reading passage.

Question 24

There is more than one reference to 2020, and one of them is indirect (you have to identify the year from what is written).

Question 25

There is an article (the) in front of the space, so the answer is a noun.

Question 26

To find where the answer is, look for a phrase which has a similar meaning to 'business leaders'.

Businesses in the 21st century

It is generally agreed that changes are taking place more quickly now, and that organisations are being transformed. One leading economist suggested that by 2020, up to a quarter of employees would be **24** .... , and half of all employees would be based in the **25** .... Although predictions can be wrong, the speed of change is not in doubt, and business leaders need to understand the **26** .... that will be influential.

The creation of lasting memories

Many studies of the brain processes underlying the creation of memory consolidation (lasting memories) have involved giving various human and animal subjects treatment, while training them to perform a task. These have contributed greatly to our understanding.

In pioneering studies using goldfish, Bernard Agranoff found that protein synthesis inhibitors* injected after training caused the goldfish to forget what they had learned. In other experiments, he administered protein synthesis inhibitors immediately before the fish were trained. The remarkable finding was that the fish learned the task completely normally, but forgot it within a few hours – that is, the protein synthesis inhibitors blocked memory consolidation, but did not influence short-term memory.

There is now extensive evidence that short-term memory is spared by many kinds of treatments, including electro-convulsive therapy (ECT), that block memory consolidation. On the other hand, and equally importantly, neuroscientist Ivan Izquierdo found that many drug treatments can block short-term memory without blocking memory consolidation. Contrary to the hypothesis put forward by Canadian psychologist Donald Hebb, in 1949, long-term memory does not require short-term memory, and vice versa.

Such findings suggest that our experiences create parallel, and possibly independent stages of memory, each with a different life span. All of this evidence from clinical and experimental studies strongly indicates that the brain handles recent and remote memory in different ways; but why does it do that?

* substances which stop or slow the growth of cells

We obviously need to have memory that is created rapidly: reacting to an ever and rapidly changing environment requires that. For example, most current building codes require that the heights of all steps in a staircase be equal. After taking a couple of steps, up or down, we implicitly remember the heights of the steps and assume that the others will be the same. If they are not the same, we are very likely to trip and fall. Lack of this kind of rapidly created implicit memory would be bad for us and for insurance companies, but perhaps good for lawyers. It would be of little value to us if we remembered the heights of the steps only after a delay of many hours, when the memory becomes consolidated.

The hypothesis that lasting memory consolidates slowly over time is supported primarily by clinical and experimental evidence that the formation of long-term memory is influenced by treatments and disorders affecting brain functioning. There are also other kinds of evidence indicating more directly that the memories consolidate over time after learning. Avi Kami and Dov Sagi reported that the performance of human subjects trained in a visual skill did not improve until eight hours after the training was completed, and that improvement was even greater the following day. Furthermore, the skill was retained for several years.

Studies using human brain imaging to study changes in neural activity induced by learning have also reported that the changes continue to develop for hours after learning. In an innovative study using functional imaging of the brain, Reza Shadmehr and Henry Holcomb examined brain activity in several brain regions shortly after human subjects were trained in a motor learning task requiring arm and hand movements. They found that while the performance of the subjects remained stable for several hours after completion of the training, their brain activity did not; different regions of the brain were predominantly active at different times over a period of several hours after the training. The activity shifted from the prefrontal cortex to two areas known to be involved in controlling movements, the motor cortex and cerebellar cortex. Consolidation of the motor skill appeared to involve activation of different neural systems that increased the stability of the brain processes underlying the skill.

There is also evidence that learning-induced changes in the activity of neurons in the cerebral cortex continue to increase for many days after the training. In an extensive series of studies using rats with electrodes implanted in the auditory cortex, Norman Weinberger reported that, after a tone of specific frequency was paired a few times with footshock, neurons in the rats' auditory cortex responded more to that specific tone and less to other tones of other frequencies. Even more interestingly, the selectivity of the neurons' response to the specific tone used in training continued to increase for several days after the training was terminated.

It is not intuitively obvious why our lasting memories consolidate slowly. Certainly, one can wonder why we have a form of memory that we have to rely on for many hours, days or a lifetime, that is so susceptible to disruption shortly after it is initiated. Perhaps the brain system that consolidates long-term memory over time was a late development in vertebrate evolution. Moreover, maybe we consolidate memories slowly because our mammalian brains are large and enormously complex. We can readily reject these ideas. All species of animals studied to date have both short and long-term memory; and all are susceptible to retrograde amnesia. Like humans, birds, bees, and molluscs, as well as fish and rats, make long-term memory slowly. Consolidation of memory clearly emerged early in evolution, and was conserved.

Although there seems to be no compelling reason to conclude that a biological system such as a brain could not quickly make a lasting memory, the fact is that animal brains do not. Thus, memory consolidation must serve some very important adaptive function or functions. There is considerable evidence suggesting that the slow consolidation is adaptive because it enables neurobiological processes occurring shortly after learning to influence the strength of memory for experiences. The extensive evidence that memory can be enhanced, as well as impaired, by treatments administered shortly after training, provides intriguing support for this hypothesis.

Questions 27–40

Questions 27–31

*Choose the correct letter, **A**, **B**, **C** or **D**.*

27 Experiments by Bernard Agranoff described in Reading Passage 3 involved
 A injecting goldfish at different stages of the experiments.
 B training goldfish to do different types of task.
 C using different types of treatment on goldfish.
 D comparing the performance of different goldfish on certain tasks.

28 Most findings from recent studies suggest that
 A drug treatments do not normally affect short-term memories.
 B long-term memories build upon short-term memories.
 C short and long-term memories are formed by separate processes.
 D ECT treatment affects both short-and long-term memories.

29 In the fifth paragraph, what does the writer want to show by the example
 of staircases?
 A Prompt memory formation underlies the performance of everyday tasks.
 B Routine tasks can be carried out unconsciously.
 C Physical accidents can impair the function of memory.
 D Complex information such as regulations cannot be retained by
   the memory.

30 Observations about memory by Kami and Sagi
 A cast doubt on existing hypotheses.
 B related only to short-term memory.
 C were based on tasks involving hearing.
 D confirmed other experimental findings.

31 What did the experiment by Shadmehr and Holcomb show?
 A Different areas of the brain were activated by different tasks.
 B Activity in the brain gradually moved from one area to other areas.
 C Subjects continued to get better at a task after training had finished.
 D Treatment given to subjects improved their performance on a task.

Questions 32–36

Do the following statements agree with the views of the writer in Reading Passage 3?

Write

YES   if the statement agrees with the views of the writer
NO   if the statement contradicts the views of the writer
NOT GIVEN   if it is impossible to say what the writer thinks about this

32 The training which Kami and Sagi's subjects were given was repeated over several days.

33 The rats in Weinberger's studies learned to associate a certain sound with a specific experience.

34 The results of Weinberger's studies indicated that the strength of the rats' learned associations increases with time.

35 It is easy to see the evolutionary advantage of the way lasting memories in humans are created.

36 Long-term memories in humans are more stable than in many other species.

Questions 37–40

Complete the summary using the list of words, **A–I**, below.

Long-term memory

Various researchers have examined the way lasting memories are formed. Laboratory experiments usually involve teaching subjects to do something **37** .... , and treating them with mild electric shocks or drugs. Other studies monitor behaviour after a learning experience, or use sophisticated equipment to observe brain activity.

The results are generally consistent: they show that lasting memories are the result of a **38** .... and complex biological process.

The fact that humans share this trait with other species, including animals with **39** .... brains, suggests that it developed **40** .... in our evolutionary history.

A early	**B** easy	**C** large	**D** late	**E** lengthy
F new	**G** recently	**H** small	**I** quick	

Writing module (1 hour)

Guidance

Overview

The Academic Writing test lasts for an hour, and consists of two parts. The first part is shorter than the second, and carries only one third of the marks, so you should spend about 20 minutes on this part and 40 minutes on the second part.

For each part you should allow enough time to plan what you are going to say before you begin writing, and to check what you have written afterwards.

Tasks

Task 1

In the first part, you have to write a minimum of 150 words altogether. You are presented with a visual which you have to describe in words, providing a general overview with supporting details. The visual might be a line graph, a bar chart, a pie chart, a diagram or a plan, and the subject of the visuals are varied. Subjects might include social trends, economics, natural or industrial processes, or health, but you do not need any specialist knowledge to do the task.

You are expected to write in a neutral or formal style.

Task 2

In the second part, you have to write an essay with a minimum of 250 words. This involves commenting on an issue or problem which is presented in the task. You are expected to discuss various points of view and arrive at a conclusion. Topics are varied, and might include health, lifestyles, environment, or education, but you do not have to have any special knowledge to be able to do the task.

You are expected to write in a neutral or formal style.

You should spend about 20 minutes on this task.

> **The table below shows the results of surveys in 2000, 2005 and 2010 about one university.**
>
> **Summarise the information by selecting and reporting the main features, and make comparisons where relevant.**

Write at least 150 words.

Percentage of students giving good ratings for different aspects of a university			
	2000	2005	2010
Teaching quality	65	63	69
Print resources	87	89	88
Electronic resources	45	72	88
Range of modules offered	32	30	27
Buildings/teaching facilities	77	77	77

Tip strip

- Make sure you understand exactly what the visual shows. In this task, the figures in the table:
  - relate to just one university,
  - are from three different surveys,
  - indicate changes in student attitudes.

You get this key information from two sources: the first sentence of the task itself and the title of the visual(s).

- For Task 1, the second part of the rubric is always the same.

- Start with an introductory sentence which summarises what the visual shows. Don't simply copy down what's in the rubric – this is a waste of your time.

- Take some time before you start writing to look for any improvements, reductions, fluctuations and similarities.

Report the most striking point first. In this task, it is probably that there was a great improvement in students' opinions of the university's electronic resources.

- Give data to support the claims you make – citing specific percentages. But you don't need to quote exact figures for every point – you will gain marks for showing that you can be selective.

- Don't write too much: 150–200 words will be enough. You won't be given any extra marks for writing a longer piece, and you need to leave enough time for Task 2.

You should spend about 40 minutes on this task.

Write about the following topic:

> **Some say that because many people are living much longer, the age at which people retire from work should be raised considerably.**
>
> **To what extent do you agree or disagree?**

Give reasons for your answer and include any relevant examples from your own knowledge and experience.

Write at least 250 words.

Tip strip

- Be clear which specific aspect of the task you need to discuss. In this task, you need to talk about whether the age of retirement should be raised and if so, whether it should be by a small or large amount.

- The second line of the task in Task 2 differs from paper to paper.

- You could give your point of view and then provide illustrations and evidence to support this opinion. Or, you could explore both sides of the question and then go on to give your own opinion and explain the arguments you find particularly persuasive.

- Write using paragraphs and make sure each paragraph has a clear central topic.

Speaking module (11–14 minutes)

Guidance

Overview

The speaking test lasts for 11–14 minutes, and it consists of three parts:

- **Part 1** takes the form of a dialogue with the examiner, who asks questions about you, your life, and things you are familiar with. It lasts for four to five minutes.
- **Part 2** is a short presentation given by you about a <u>general</u> topic that the examiner chooses. You can decide the <u>specific</u> topic yourself. The topic is connected to your own life and experiences.

You have up to one minute to prepare your presentation, and you can speak for up to two minutes. There is a clock on the table, and the examiner reminds you of the timing if necessary.

- **Part 3** takes the form of a dialogue with the examiner. He/she asks you about your views on impersonal subjects which are loosely connected to the topic of your presentation. This lasts between four and five minutes.

Tasks

- In **Part 1**, the questions which the examiner asks you are usually factual, and quite simple, such as 'When …?', 'Who …?', 'How often …?', or 'What kind of …?'
- In **Part 2**, you will be given a candidate card.
  - The topic of your presentation is outlined in the first line of the candidate card. It starts with 'Describe …'.
  - You may be asked about something that happened in the past, or someone you know, or something you would like to do in the future.
  - Three separate bullet points tell you what to include in your presentation, and a fourth line tells you to explain something in more detail, such as your feelings, or the reason for something.
- In **Part 3**, the questions that the examiner asks you are more complex, and involve lengthier responses. You may be asked 'What is your opinion about …?'; 'To what extent do you think …?'; 'How important is it to …?'; compared to 'What do you think …?'; or 'What might the reason be for …?'

Tip strip

Your country …

• **Question 1** Remember that 'What's the … like?' means 'Describe'.

• **Questions 2–3** Give a reason for your answer.

Your family …

Question 4 Don't spend a long time deciding who to talk about.

Answer these questions.

Tell me about your country.

What's the weather like in your country?
Which time of year do you think is best in your country? Why?
Have you visited many different parts of your country? Why/Why not?

Now let's talk about your family.

Do you share a house with any of your family? Who?
Do most people in your family live in the same town or village?
When did you last have a family party?
Which person in your family are you most similar to? How?

Tip strip

• Choose a place that you can talk about easily.

• It is all right to spend more time on one bullet than on others.

• Don't forget to include the last line ('and explain…') in your presentation.

You have one minute to make notes on the following topic. Then you have up to two minutes to talk about it.

> Describe a place in another part of the world that you would love to visit in the future.
>
> You should say:
>
> > what you know about the place
> > how you know about it
> > how you would go there
>
> and explain why you would love to visit that place.

Who would you go to that place with?
Do you enjoy travelling generally?

Tip strip

TV programmes …

• If you don't understand the question, ask the examiner to repeat or explain it.

Other countries …

• Listen carefully to what the examiner says he/she wants to talk about.

• **Question 2** It doesn't matter whether you agree or disagree with this opinion, but give as many reasons and examples as you can.

The tourism industry …

• **Question 1** If you don't know the answer, you can guess. If you don't want to guess, tell the examiner that you don't know much about this subject.

• **Question 2** Ask for help if there's a word you don't understand.

Consider these questions and then answer them.

Let's go on to discuss TV programmes about other places.

What kinds of TV programme about different places are most popular in your country?
Can people learn more about geography from TV than they can from books? Why/Why not?
Do you think TV programmes about different places encourage people to travel themselves? Why/Why not?

Now let's talk about visiting other countries.

For what reasons do you think international travel has increased in recent years?
Some people say it's important for people to find out about another country before they visit it. Do you agree?
How useful is it for people to understand the language of the countries they visit? Why?

Now let's consider the tourism industry.

Does tourism play a big part in the economy of your country? How?
What kinds of unpredictable factors can have a negative effect on the tourism industry?
In the future, what kinds of development might there be in the tourism industry?

TEST 2

Listening module (approx 30 minutes + 10 minutes transfer time)

SECTION 1

Guidance

Focus

- In **Section 1**, the focus is on listening for facts in a conversation (social context).
- In **Section 2**, the focus is on listening for facts in a talk or presentation (social context).
- In **Section 3**, the focus is on listening for in a conversation (2–3 people) facts and opinions (education/training context).
- In **Section 4**, the focus is on listening for specific details and main ideas in a lecture, in an education/training context.

Preparation Tips

General preparation

Although you cannot predict exactly the language which the IELTS test will contain, there are several ways you can prepare for taking the listening test.

- Do plenty of IELTS listening practice tests – listen to the recording only once and try to build up your confidence for taking the real test.
- Aim to listen to spoken English in a wide variety of situations and topic areas. Listen to CDs, radio, TV and Internet broadcasts featuring native speakers of English. Don't worry if you don't catch every word, you'll understand more with practice.

Preparation for specific sections

- To help prepare you for Sections 1 and 3 (two or more people interacting); if you live in a country where English is spoken, try to listen to people conversing, particularly in 'transactional situations' (where people are trying to get something done), e.g. in shops, hotels, clinics. Also try to engage people in conversation yourself. Listen for particular phrases which signal key elements, such as a speaker's opinion or which point is being emphasised.
- To help prepare for Sections 2 and 4, ('long turn' monologues, with one person speaking for some time without interacting with others), try to listen to podcasts on the Internet and more formal talk shows on radio channels like the British Broadcasting Corporation (BBC) Radio 4 or the Voice of America (VOA).

Strategies

- Practise reading the question paper quickly, getting a clear idea of what you are required to listen for.
- Use the 'context' information to help you identify the correct answer. Listen carefully to the information provided at the beginning of each section, telling you who is speaking, in what situation and for what purpose.
- IELTS recordings are only played ONCE, so it's important you don't worry too much if you miss the answer to one question. Move on and listen for the answer to the next question. Try to look for 'clues' on the question paper, e.g. any sub–headings, or paraphrases of what you hear. This will prevent you from 'losing your place'.
- As with all parts of the IELTS, if you aren't sure of the answer take a guess. You won't lose marks for a wrong answer; and using 'context' information can often help you make a successful prediction.

Questions 1–10

Questions 1–10

Complete the form below.

Write **NO MORE THAN TWO WORDS AND/OR A NUMBER** for each answer.

Tip strip

Questions 1–10

Read the form carefully before you listen. You will be able to get a lot of useful information about the context (an animal park), purpose of the phone call (temporary job enquiry) and who is completing the form (a receptionist at the park).

Question 1

Listen carefully to the discussion about the spelling of the surname: the man thinks there is a double letter in her name, but the woman corrects him.

Question 2

For **Task 1**, you often have to write down an address. If addresses are not spelt out (as in this case), they contain very familiar nouns.

Question 3

Listen for a date. Several are mentioned, but listen carefully for the relevant one. It is expressed in the negative 'I can't start work until …'.

Question 9

There are different ways of saying '0' in phone numbers: you can say 'zero' or 'oh'. Also, listen for 'double' numbers.

Question 10

Listen for a type of minor disability.

Pinder's Animal Park

Example

Enquiries about <u>temporary</u> work

Personal Details:

Name: Jane **1** ………………

Address: **2** ………………

                                        Exeter

Telephone number: 07792430921

Availability: Can start work on **3** ………………

Work details:

Preferred type of work: Assistant **4** ………………

Relevant skills: Familiar with kitchen **5** ………………

Relevant qualifications: A **6** ……………… certificate

Training required: A **7** ……………… course

Referee:

Name: Dr Ruth Price

Position: **8** ………………

Phone number: **9** ………………

Other: Applicant has a form of **10** ………………

Questions 11–20

Tip strip
Questions 11–15
For multiple choice questions in Task 2, you might have to listen for the main idea as well as specific details. You will also sometimes have to listen for people's opinions.
Question 12
Listen for the opinion of the previous year's group and for a past time reference.

Questions 11–15

*Choose the correct answer, **A**, **B** or **C**.*

Tamerton Centre

11 The Tamerton Centre was set up in order to encourage people

    A to enjoy being in the countryside.

    B to help conserve the countryside.

    C to learn more about the countryside.

12 Last year's group said that the course

    A built their self esteem.

    B taught them lots of new skills.

    C made them fitter and stronger.

13 For the speaker, what's the most special feature of the course?

    A You can choose which activities you do.

    B There's such a wide variety of activities.

    C You can become an expert in new activities.

14 The speaker advises people to bring

    A their own board games.

    B extra table tennis equipment.

    C a selection of films on DVD.

15 Bed-time is strictly enforced because

    A it's a way to reduce bad behaviour.

    B tiredness can lead to accidents.

    C it makes it easy to check everyone's in.

Questions 16–20

Tip strip
Questions 16–20
The speaker talks about five different objects and there are just three options to choose from. You must listen for which objects are <u>required</u> in the Centre, which are <u>allowed</u> and which are definitely <u>not allowed</u>.

• In this type of task, you can use each option more than once.

• Listen for phrases with modals such as – 'you don't have to …', 'they're a must …', 'you can if you wish …', as well as adjectives like 'banned'.

What rules apply to taking different objects to the Centre?

*Match each object with the correct rule, **A–C**.*

*Write the correct letter, **A–C**.*

Objects

16 Electrical equipment ....

17 Mobile phone ....

18 Sun cream ....

19 Aerosol deodorant ....

20 Towel ....

Rules

  A You MUST take this

  B You CAN take this, if you wish

  C You must NOT take this

Questions 21–30

Tip strip

Questions 21–30

Listen carefully to the context information, it will help you understand the setting better. This conversation features a student teacher talking through her plans for two different lessons with her tutor.

Questions 21–25

• You use each option only once and two options will not be used.

• The speaker mentions five different parts of the plant in the order they appear on the question paper (Questions 21–25), and describes their position and/or shape and function.

• Listen for prepositions and direction indicators such as 'on the left', 'at the top', and 'on the bottom'. Also, listen for words which indicate shape and size.

Questions 21–25

Label the diagram below.

*Write the correct letter, **A–G**, next to questions 21–25 below.*

(Year 6 Lesson)   **Biogas Plant**

21	Waste container	....
22	Slurry	....
23	Water inlet	....
24	Gas	....
25	Overflow tank	....

Complete the flow chart below.

Choose **FIVE** answers from the box and write the correct letter, **A–G**, next to questions 26–30.

Tip strip
Questions 26–30
During the pause in the middle of the recording, read Questions 26–30. It is important to know who is doing what. Questions 26, 27 and 30 are the teacher's activities but Questions 28 and 29 are the pupils' activities.

A	Identify sequence.
B	Ask questions.
C	Copy.
D	Demonstrate meaning.
E	Distribute worksheet.
F	Draw pictures.
G	Present sentences.

LESSON OUTLINE YEAR THREE
TOPIC: ENERGY

ACTIVITIES

Teacher: Introduce word
Pupils: look and listen

Teacher: **26** ………………
Pupils: look and listen

Teacher: Present question
Pupils: respond

Teacher: **27** ………………
*Pupils: **28** ……………… and expand*

Teacher: Display pictures
*Pupils: **29** ………………*

Teacher: **30** ………………
Pupils: write

Teacher: Monitor pupils

Questions 31–40

Questions 31–40

Complete the notes below.

Write **NO MORE THAN TWO WORDS** for each answer.

Tip strip

Questions 31–40

- Section 4 lectures often deal with quite technical matters, but speakers give simple and clear definitions to make things clear for a non-specialist audience. Listen to the short definition of 'artificial gills' in the instructions and also the background information at the beginning of the lecture.

- Before you listen, read all the notes on the question paper (remember there is no pause in the middle of Section 4). The notes on the paper give a lot of information to help you understand the main points and also enable you to 'find your place' on the paper.

- There is quite a long introduction before the first question. Read the first two bullet points (without gaps) as you listen. This will prepare you to hear the answer to Question 31.

Question 31

Listen for a synonym for 'large'.

Question 32

Listen for the cue '1960s'.

Question 33

Listen for the cues: 'animals without gills' and 'bubbles'.

Question 38

Listen for the cue: 'limitation'.

Creating artificial gills

Background

- *Taking in oxygen : mammals – lungs; fish – gills*

- *Long-held dreams – humans swimming underwater without oxygen tanks*

- *Oxygen tanks considered too* **31** .... *and large*

- *Attempts to extract oxygen directly from water*

- *1960s – prediction that humans would have gills added by* **32** ....

- *Ideas for artificial gills were inspired by research on*

  - *fish gills*

  - *fish swim bladders*

  - *animals without gills – especially bubbles used by* **33** ....

Building a simple artificial gill

- *Make a watertight box of a material which lets* **34** .... *pass through*

- *Fill with air and submerge in water*

- *Important that the diver and the water keep* **35** ....

- *The gill has to have a large* **36** ....

- *Designers often use a network of small* **37** .... *on their gill*

  Main limitation – problems caused by increased **38** .... *in deeper water*

Other applications

- *Supplying oxygen for use on* **39** ....

- *Powering* **40** .... *cells for driving machinery underwater*

Reading module (1 hour)

Guidance

Focus

- Reading for main ideas.
- Reading for detail.
- Skim reading.
- Understanding a sequence of ideas.
- Recognising writers' opinions, attitudes and inferences.

Preparation Tips

- As the IELTS test is a proficiency test, it is not based on a specific language syllabus. This means that you cannot predict exactly the language which the test will contain.
- Aim to improve your general language knowledge and skills, as well as to develop effective strategies.
- Aim to read appropriate materials about a wide range of topics as often as possible. Even academic texts about different subjects have a high proportion of words and structures in common.
- Try also to increase your reading speed. The length of time allowed for each section of the reading test is relatively short, so you will need to be able to read the texts and the questions quickly.
- Over time, your general proficiency in English will increase and your potential test performance will rise.

Strategies

- When you are preparing to take the Academic Reading test, you should try to develop strategies for doing the test which work well for you. Some strategies are useful for most people, but in other cases what works well for one person might not work so well for another. For example, some people find it best to read each text quickly *before* attempting to do the tasks, while others simply skim the text and then read parts of it selectively *at the same time* as they are doing the tasks.
- The types of task found in the Academic Reading test are limited, so although you cannot predict exactly which ones a test might contain, you will be able to familiarise yourself with all the possible task types. It is very important that you know what to expect in general, and have practised doing the tasks before you do the test. You will be able to develop strategies for doing the tasks which work best for you.
- One strategy which benefits most people is the use of guesswork. When you are reading the texts and questions, you will almost certainly come across words and phrases which you are unfamiliar with. Use the context, as well as your knowledge of any other English words that are similar, to guess their meaning. If you come across a question which you find particularly difficult, move on to the next one and then return to it later. If you still find it too difficult, guess the answer – you might get it right. You won't lose extra marks for giving a wrong answer, but you won't gain any mark if you leave a question unanswered.

Sport Science in Australia

The professional career paths available to graduates from courses relating to human movement and sport science are as diverse as the graduate's imagination. However, undergraduate courses with this type of content, in Australia as well as in most other Western countries, were originally designed as preparation programmes for Physical Education (PE) teachers.

The initial programmes commenced soon after the conclusion of World War II in the mid-1940s. One of the primary motives for these initiatives was the fact that, during the war effort, so many of the men who were assessed for military duty had been declared unfit. The government saw the solution in the providing of Physical Education programmes in schools, delivered by better prepared and specifically educated PE teachers.

Later, in the 1970s and early 1980s, the surplus of Australians graduating with a PE degree obliged institutions delivering this qualification to identify new employment opportunities for their graduates, resulting in the first appearance of degrees catering for recreation professionals. In many instances, this diversity of programme delivery merely led to degrees, delivered by physical educators, as a side-line activity to the production of PE teachers.

Whilst the need to produce Physical Education teachers remains a significant social need, and most developed societies demand the availability of quality leisure programmes for their citizens, the career options of graduates within this domain are still developing. The two most evident growth domains are in the area of the professional delivery of sport, and the role of a physical lifestyle for community health.

The sports industry is developing at an unprecedented rate of growth. From a business perspective, sport is now seen as an area with the potential for high returns. It is quite significant that the businessman Rupert Murdoch broadened his business base from media to sport, having purchased an American baseball team and an Australian Rugby League competition, as well as seeking opportunities to invest in an English football club. No business person of such international stature would see fit to invest in sport unless he was satisfied that this was a sound business venture with ideal revenue-generating opportunities.

These developments have confirmed sport as a business with professional management structures, marketing processes, and development strategies in place. They have indicated new and developing career paths for graduates of human movement science, sport science, exercise science and related degrees. Graduates can now visualise career paths extending into such diverse domains as sport management, sport marketing, event and facility management, government policy development pertaining to sport, sport journalism, sport psychology, and sport or athletic coaching.

Business leaders will only continue their enthusiasm for sport if they receive returns for their money. Such returns will only be forthcoming if astute, enthusiastic and properly educated professionals are delivering the programs that earn appropriate financial returns. The successful universities of the 21st century will be those that have responded to this challenge by delivering such degrees.

A second professional growth area for this group of graduates is associated with community health. The increasing demand for government expenditure within health budgets is reaching the stage where most governments are simply unable to function in a manner that is satisfying their constituents. One of the primary reasons for this problem is the unhelpful emphasis on treatment in medical care programmes. Governments have traditionally given their senior health official the title of 'Minister for Health', when in fact this officer has functioned as 'Minister for Sickness and the Construction of Hospitals'. Government focus simply has to change. If the change is not brought about for philosophical reasons, it will occur naturally, because insufficient funding will be available to address the ever-increasing costs of medical support.

Graduates of human movement, exercise science and sport science have the potential to become major players in this shift in policy focus. It is these graduates who already have the skills, knowledge and understanding to initiate community health education programmes to reduce cardio-vascular disease, to reduce medical dependency upon diabetes, to improve workplace health leading to increased productivity, to initiate and promote programmes of activity for the elderly that reduce medical dependency, and to maintain an active lifestyle for the unemployed and disadvantaged groups in society. This is the graduate that governments will be calling upon to shift the community focus from medical dependency to healthy lifestyles in the decades ahead.

The career paths of these graduates are developing at a pace that is not evident in other professions. The contribution that these graduates can make to society, and the recognition of this contribution is at an unprecedented high, and all indications are that it will continue to grow.

Complete the flow chart below.

Choose **NO MORE THAN TWO WORDS** from the passage for each answer.

The history of sports and physical science in Australia

A lot of people identified as being **1** ....

↓

Introduction of PE to **2** ....

↓

Special training programmes for **3** ....

↓

4 .... of PE graduates

↓

Identification of alternative **5** ....

↓

Diversification of course delivery

Tip strip

Questions 1–5

- The title of the flow chart shows that it's about the past, so look for the answers in the first three paragraphs.

- Write *either* one word *or* two words for the answers, but no more.

- Make sure that the answers fit grammatically as well as in meaning.

- The answers follow the order of information in the reading passage.

- The last box is useful. It shows you where the relevant part of the reading passage ends.

- If you have to change a word or phrase to make it fit, you have chosen the wrong one.

Question 1

'Being' comes before the space, so the answer must be an adjective or an adverb.

Question 5

'Alternative' comes in front of the space, and there is no article, so the answer is either an uncountable or a plural noun phrase.

Questions 6–13

Do the following statements agree with the information given in Reading Passage 1?

Write

TRUE   if the statement agrees with the information
FALSE   if the statement contradicts the information
NOT GIVEN   if there is no information on this

Tip strip
Questions 6–13

• There's no need to answer the questions in words. Just write *T*, or *F*, or *NG*.

• The statements follow the order of the information in the reading passage.

• To find the part of the reading passage which contains the answer, look for words and phrases with similar meanings.

• Read each *complete* statement before deciding the answers.

Question 13

This statement sounds reasonable in the light of what is said in the reading passage, and *may* be true. However, it must be stated by the writer for it to be definitely true.

6   Sport is generally regarded as a profitable area for investment.

7   Rupert Murdoch has a personal as well as a business interest in sport.

8   The range of career opportunities available to sport graduates is increasing.

9   The interests of business and the interests of universities are linked.

10 Governments have been focusing too much attention on preventative medicine.

11 It is inevitable that government priorities for health spending will change.

12 Existing degree courses are unsuitable for careers in community health.

13 Funding for sport science and related degrees has been increased considerably.

An assessment of micro-wind turbines

A In terms of micro-renewable energy sources suitable for private use, a 15-kilowatt (kW) turbine* is at the biggest end of the spectrum. With a nine metre diameter and a pole as high as a four-storey house, this is the most efficient form of wind micro-turbine, and the sort of thing you could install only if you had plenty of space and money. According to one estimate, a 15-kW micro-turbine (that's one with the maximum output), costing £41,000 to purchase and a further £9,000 to install, is capable of delivering 25,000 kilowatt-hours (kWh)** of electricity each year if placed on a suitably windy site.

B I don't know of any credible studies of the greenhouse gas emissions involved in producing and installing turbines, so my estimates here are going to be even more broad than usual. However, it is worth trying. If turbine manufacture is about as carbon intensive per pound sterling of product as other generators and electrical motors, which seems a reasonable assumption, the carbon intensity of manufacture will be around 640 kilograms (kg) per £1,000 of value. Installation is probably about as carbon intensive as typical construction, at around 380 kg per £1,000. That makes the carbon footprint (the total amount of greenhouse gases that installing a turbine creates) 30 tonnes.

C The carbon savings from wind-powered electricity generation depend on the carbon intensity of the electricity that you're replacing. Let's assume that your generation replaces the coal-fuelled part of the country's energy mix. In other words, if you live in the UK, let's say that rather than replacing typical grid electricity, which comes from a mix of coal, gas, oil and renewable energy sources, the effect of your turbine is to reduce the use of coal-fired power stations. That's reasonable, because coal is the least preferable source in the electricity mix. In this case the carbon saving is roughly one kilogram per kWh, so you save 25 tonnes per year and pay back the embodied carbon in just 14 months – a great start.

D The UK government has recently introduced a subsidy for renewable energy that pays individual producers 24p per energy unit on top of all the money they save on their own fuel bill, and on selling surplus electricity back to the grid at approximately 5p per unit. With all this taken into account, individuals would get back £7,250 per year on their investment. That pays back the costs in about six years. It makes good financial sense and, for people who care about the carbon savings for their own sake, it looks like a fantastic move. The carbon investment pays back in just over a year, and every year after that is a 25-tonne carbon saving. (It's important to remember that all these sums rely on a wind turbine having a favourable location.)

E So, at face value, the turbine looks like a great idea environmentally, and a fairly good long-term investment economically for the person installing it. However, there is a crucial perspective missing from the analysis so far. Has the government spent its money wisely? It has invested 24p per unit into each micro-turbine. That works out at a massive £250 per tonne of carbon saved. My calculations tell me that had the government invested its money in offshore wind farms, instead of subsidising smaller domestic turbines, they would have broken even after eight years. In other words, the micro-turbine works out as a good investment for individuals, but only because the government spends, and arguably wastes, so much money subsidising it. Carbon savings are far lower too.

F Nevertheless, although the micro-wind turbine subsidy doesn't look like the very best way of spending government resources on climate change mitigation, we are talking about investing only about 0.075 percent per year of the nation's GDP to get a one percent reduction in carbon emissions, which is a worthwhile benefit. In other words, it could be much better, but it could be worse. In addition, such investment helps to promote and sustain developing technology.

G There is one extra favourable way of looking at the micro-wind turbine, even if it is not the single best way of investing money in cutting carbon. Input-output modelling has told us that it is actually quite difficult to spend money without having a negative carbon impact. So if the subsidy encourages people to spend their money on a carbon-reducing technology such as a wind turbine, rather than on carbon-producing goods like cars, and services such as overseas holidays, then the reductions in emissions will be greater than my simple sums above have suggested.

---

*   a type of engine

**   a unit for measuring electrical power

Questions 14–26

Questions 14–20

Reading Passage 2 has **SEVEN** paragraphs, **A–G**.

Choose the correct heading for each paragraph from the list of headings below.

Write the correct number, **i–ix**.

List of Headings

i   A better use for large sums of money.

ii   The environmental costs of manufacture and installation.

iii Estimates of the number of micro-turbines in use.

iv   The environmental benefits of running a micro-turbine.

v   The size and output of the largest type of micro-turbine.

vi   A limited case for subsidising micro-turbines.

vii Recent improvements in the design of micro-turbines.

viii An indirect method of reducing carbon emissions.

ix   The financial benefits of running a micro-turbine.

---

14 Paragraph **A** ....

15 Paragraph **B** ....

16 Paragraph **C** ....

17 Paragraph **D** ....

18 Paragraph **E** ....

19 Paragraph **F** ....

20 Paragraph **G** ....

Tip strip

Questions 21–22

- *Don't* choose statements because *you* agree with them. Only choose statements which are made by the writer of the reading passage.

- Only two statements are correct.

- In the Reading test, the options are in the same order as the information in the reading passage.

- For each statement, find the part of the passage which is most likely to contain the answer.

Choose **TWO** letters, **A–E**.

The list below contains some possible statements about micro wind-turbines.

Which **TWO** of these statements are made by the writer of the passage?

    A In certain areas, permission is required to install them.

    B Their exact energy output depends on their position.

    C They probably take less energy to make than other engines.

    D The UK government contributes towards their purchase cost.

    E They can produce more energy than a household needs.

Questions 23–26

Complete the sentences below.

Choose **NO MORE THAN THREE WORDS** *from the passage for each answer.*

23 ……………… would be a more effective target for government investment than micro-turbines.

24 An indirect benefit of subsidising micro-turbines is the support it provides for ……………… .

25 Most spending has a ……………… effect on the environment.

26 If people buy a micro-turbine, they have less money to spend on things like foreign holidays and ……………… .

Tip strip

Question 23–26

- The sentences follow the order of information in the reading passage, so when you've found the part where the first one is, you can find the rest more easily.

- If the maximum number of words is three, it's likely that at least one answer will contain three words.

- Read the whole sentence carefully before choosing an answer.

- Copy the words carefully, especially when copying words which you aren't familiar with. Check the spelling afterwards.

Question 23

The sentence compares micro-turbines with something else. The answer must be a noun phrase.

Question 25

The word after the space is a noun, and the word before the space is 'a', so the answer must be an adjective beginning with a consonant.

READING PASSAGE 3

You should spend about 20 minutes on **Questions 27–40**, which are based on Reading Passage 3 below.

Pottery production in ancient Akrotiri

Excavations at the site of prehistoric Akrotiri, on the coast of the Aegean Sea, have revealed much about the technical aspects of pottery manufacture, indisputably one of the basic industries of this Greek city. However, considerably less is known about the socio-economic context and the way production was organised.

The bulk of pottery found at Akrotiri is locally made, and dates from the late fifteenth century BC. It clearly fulfilled a vast range of the settlement's requirements: more than fifty different types of pots can be distinguished. The pottery found includes a wide variety of functional types like storage jars, smaller containers, pouring vessels, cooking pots, drinking vessels and so on, which all relate to specific activities and which would have been made and distributed with those activities in mind. Given the large number of shapes produced and the relatively high degree of standardisation, it has generally been assumed that most, if not all, of Akrotiri pottery was produced by specialised craftsmen in a non-domestic context. Unfortunately neither the potters' workshops nor kilns have been found within the excavated area. The reason may be that the ceramic workshops were located on the periphery of the site, which has not yet been excavated. In any event, the ubiquity of the pottery, and the consistent repetition of the same types in different sizes, suggests production on an industrial scale.

The Akrotirian potters seem to have responded to pressures beyond their households, namely to the increasing complexity of regional distribution and exchange systems. We can imagine them as full-time craftsmen working permanently in a high production-rate craft such as pottery manufacture, and supporting themselves entirely from the proceeds of their craft. In view of the above, one can begin to speak in terms of mass-produced pottery and the existence of organised workshops of craftsmen during the period 1550–1500 BC. Yet, how pottery production was organised at Akrotiri remains an open question, as there is no real documentary evidence. Our entire knowledge comes from the ceramic material itself, and the tentative conclusions which can be drawn from it.

The invention of units of quantity and of a numerical system to count them was of capital importance for an exchange-geared society such as that of Akrotiri. In spite of the absence of any written records, the archaeological evidence reveals that concepts of measurements, both of weight and number, had been formulated. Standard measures may already have been in operation, such as those evidenced by a graduated series of lead weights – made in disc form – found at the site. The existence of units of capacity in Late Bronze Age times is also evidenced, by the notation of units of a liquid measure for wine on excavated containers.

It must be recognised that the function of pottery vessels plays a very important role in determining their characteristics. The intended function affects the choice of clay, the production technique, and the shape and the size of the pots. For example, large storage jars (*pithoi*) would be needed to store commodities, whereas smaller containers would be used for transport. In fact, the length of a man's arm limits the size of a smaller pot to a capacity of about twenty litres; that is also the maximum a man can comfortably carry.

The various sizes of container would thus represent standard quantities of a commodity, which is a fundamental element in the function of exchange. Akrotirian merchants handling a commodity such as wine would have been able to determine easily the amount of wine they were transporting from the number of containers they carried in their ships, since the capacity of each container was known to be 14–18 litres. (We could draw a parallel here with the current practice in Greece of selling oil in 17 kilogram tins.)

We may therefore assume that the shape, capacity, and, sometimes decoration of vessels are indicative of the commodity contained by them. Since individual transactions would normally involve different quantities of a given commodity, a range of 'standardised' types of vessel would be needed to meet traders' requirements.

In trying to reconstruct systems of capacity by measuring the volume of excavated pottery, a rather generous range of tolerances must be allowed. It seems possible that the potters of that time had specific sizes of vessel in mind, and tried to reproduce them using a specific type and amount of clay. However, it would be quite difficult for them to achieve the exact size required every time, without any mechanical means of regulating symmetry and wall thickness, and some potters would be more skilled than others. In addition, variations in the repetition of types and size may also occur because of unforeseen circumstances during the throwing process. For instance, instead of destroying the entire pot if the clay in the rim contained a piece of grit, a potter might produce a smaller pot by simply cutting off the rim. Even where there is no noticeable external difference between pots meant to contain the same quantity of a commodity, differences in their capacity can actually reach one or two litres. In one case the deviation from the required size appears to be as much as 10–20 percent.

The establishment of regular trade routes within the Aegean led to increased movement of goods; consequently a regular exchange of local, luxury and surplus goods, including metals, would have become feasible as a result of the advances in transport technology. The increased demand for standardised exchanges, inextricably linked to commercial transactions, might have been one of the main factors which led to the standardisation of pottery production. Thus, the whole network of ceramic production and exchange would have depended on specific regional economic conditions, and would reflect the socio-economic structure of prehistoric Akrotiri.

Questions 27–40

Tip strip
Questions 27–28

- The questions follow the order of information in the reading passage, so the answer to Question 27 can be found before the answer to Question 28.
- The information in the options *may not* follow the order of information in the reading passage.
- Some of the words and phrases in the incorrect options, or words and phrases with a similar meaning, can probably be found in the reading passage. So after you've chosen an answer, check that the other options are wrong.
- If you can't find the correct answer, and you're running out of time, it's better to guess than to leave the question unanswered.

Question 28

To find where the answer is, look for words related to 'assumption' and 'specialists', then read the following sentences carefully.

Questions 27–28

*Choose the correct letter, **A**, **B**, **C** or **D**.*

27 What does the writer say about items of pottery excavated at Akrotiri?

   A There was very little duplication.

   B They would have met a big variety of needs.

   C Most of them had been imported from other places.

   D The intended purpose of each piece was unclear.

28 The assumption that pottery from Akrotiri was produced by specialists is partly based on

   A the discovery of kilns.

   B the central location of workshops.

   C the sophistication of decorative patterns.

   D the wide range of shapes represented.

Questions 29–32

*Complete each sentence with the correct ending, **A–F**, below.*

*Write the correct letter, **A–F**.*

29 The assumption that standard units of weight were in use could be based on

30 Evidence of the use of standard units of volume is provided by

31 The size of certain types of containers would have been restricted by

32 Attempts to identify the intended capacity of containers are complicated by

   A the discovery of a collection of metal discs.

   B the size and type of the sailing ships in use.

   C variations in the exact shape and thickness of similar containers.

   D the physical characteristics of workmen.

   E marks found on wine containers.

   F the variety of commodities for which they would have been used.

Tip strip
Questions 29–32 and Questions 39–40

- Read all the options quickly before you begin the task.
- The questions follow the order of information in the reading passage.
- Each of the correct options can only be used once.

Question 30

To find where the answer is, look for a word with a similar meaning to 'volume'.

Question 32

To find where the answer is, look for a phrase with a similar meaning to 'attempts to identify the intended capacity', and then read the following sentences.

Tip strip

Questions 33–38

Don't answer the questions by using your own knowledge or opinion. Answer only according to what the writer of the passage says.

Question 40

The answer to this question can't be found in a single part of the reading passage, but the first and last paragraphs (the introduction and the conclusion) are particularly important.

Do the following statements agree with the views of the writer in Reading Passage 3?

Write

YES	if the statement agrees with the claims of the writer
NO	if the statement contradicts the claims of the writer
NOT GIVEN	if it is impossible to say what the writer thinks about this

33 There are plans to excavate new areas of the archaeological site in the near future.

34 Some of the evidence concerning pottery production in ancient Akrotiri comes from written records.

35 Pots for transporting liquids would have held no more than about 20 litres.

36 It would have been hard for merchants to calculate how much wine was on their ships.

37 The capacity of containers intended to hold the same amounts differed by up to 20 percent.

38 Regular trading of goods around the Aegean would have led to the general standardisation of quantities.

Question 39–40

Choose the correct letter, **A**, **B**, **C** or **D**.

39 What does the writer say about the standardisation of container sizes?

    A Containers which looked the same from the outside often varied in capacity.

    B The instruments used to control container size were unreliable.

    C The unsystematic use of different types of clay resulted in size variations.

    D Potters usually discarded containers which were of a non-standard size.

40 What is probably the main purpose of Reading Passage 3?

    A To evaluate the quality of pottery containers found in prehistoric Akrotiri.

    B To suggest how features of pottery production at Akrotiri reflected other developments in the region.

    C To outline the development of pottery-making skills in ancient Greece.

    D To describe methods for storing and transporting household goods in prehistoric societies.

Writing module (1 hour)

Guidance

Focus

Task 1 tests your ability to summarise the information represented in a visual, such as a graph, bar chart, pie chart, plan or diagram.

You are expected to analyse the information, and identify the main trends or patterns. You have to then summarise these, and select appropriate information to exemplify them. You do not have to mention everything which appears in the visual.

Task 2 tests your ability to write a well-organised essay on a given topic.

The topic is usually expressed in terms of a statement, followed by a question, or questions. You will be expected to summarise opposing views and offer your own opinion, or describe the reasons for a given situation and suggest possible causes or solutions.

Preparation Tips

For **Task 1**, look for samples of graphs, charts and diagrams, and practise analysing the information. You can do this in your own language; the important thing is that you are able to process visual information both accurately and quickly.

Then practise summarising the information in English.

For **Task 2**, read articles from a wide range of suitable sources and subject matter.

In addition, practise writing essays according to the process suggested in the Writing File.

While practising for both tasks, impose a time limit on yourself so that you get used to writing quickly, and have enough time left to check your essay. Also, pay attention to your handwriting. Ask other people to tell you if it is legible, and practise letter formation to improve your handwriting.

Strategies

Manage your time effectively. *Don't* spend all your time writing. Allow sufficient time to read the rubrics and, for Task 1, to analyse the visual. Also allow time to check and correct your writing afterwards.

You should spend about 20 minutes on this task.

- Start with an introductory sentence summarising what the visual shows. Don't just copy the task rubric – aim to modify/add to it slightly, to make the focus clearer.

- You are required to explain every stage of the process, but avoid repeating the same structures over and over again. Aim to use a variety of different verb forms – this will make the essay more interesting and readable.

- In process tasks particularly, it is important to use clear sequence markers, e.g. 'Firstly', 'After that …' and phrases which indicate sequence such as 'Having been cleaned…', 'On arrival they …'.

- Process tasks require you to use the passive voice for many parts of the report (e.g. 'The leather is then transported …', 'They are submerged …') because the action is more important than knowing who performed it.

The diagram below show how leather goods are produced.

Summarise the information by selecting and reporting the main features, and making comparisons where relevant.

Write at least 150 words.

A method of producing leather goods

WRITING TASK 2

You should spend about 40 minutes on this task.

Write about the following topic:

As children become adults, their social behaviour changes in some ways.

What are the main differences between young children's social behaviour and that of adults? To what extent are the changes that take place good?

Give reasons for your answer, and include any relevant examples from your own knowledge or experience.

Write at least 250 words.

Tip strip

- In this task, you must: a) explain the main differences between children's and adults' social behaviour and b) state how far you regard these changes as positive. **Note**: do not waste time discussing whether social behaviour changes. You must accept this.

- You can list all the differences in the first paragraph and then, in the second paragraph, discuss the extent to which these are positive.

  Or, you can explain the first difference and discuss whether it is good or bad, then explain the second difference and discuss whether it is positive, and so on.

Speaking module (11–14 minutes)

Guidance

Focus

The examiner assesses your speaking ability according to the same four criteria for each part of the test: relevance and coherence, vocabulary; grammar and pronunciation.

You may get a different grade for each separate criterion, but your final grade will be based on all four criteria.

- **Part 1** tests your ability to answer simple questions on familiar topics.
- **Part 2** tests your ability to speak continuously, and at length, on a familiar topic.
- **Part 3** tests your ability to converse on more abstract and impersonal topics.

Preparation Tips

- Listen to short talks and dialogues in English about everyday topics. Suitable sources would be published listening materials, as well as TV, radio or the Internet.
- Listen to longer interviews and discussions about more serious, impersonal topics, selecting from the same types of source.
- Take opportunities to talk to English speakers as often as possible. Use communication strategies to keep the conversation going if necessary.
- Practise giving short presentations about experiences you have had or people you know, etc. If possible, record yourself and listen to the recording.
- Practise giving short presentations to other people, and ask them to give you feedback.

Strategies

- While you are speaking, don't focus too much on accuracy. If you think too much about grammar, your fluency may be affected.
- If there is a word or phrase you can't remember, find other ways to say what you want to say. You are in control of the language you use in a speaking test.
- If the general topic is one you don't know much about, use your imagination. You will be assessed on how you speak, not on what you say.

PART 1

Tip strip

Free time …

- **Question 2** Give more than one answer.
- **Question 3** Say a name, and something about that person.

Clothes …

- **Question 3** If the question is in the past tense, use the past tense in your answer.
- **Question 4** This question is not about what clothes you like!

Answer these questions.

I'd like to talk to you about free time.

How much free time do you normally have? Why/Why not?
What do you usually do in your free time?
Who do you spend your free time with?
Do you wish you had more free time? Why/Why not?

Now let's discuss clothes.

Is it important to you to wear clothes that are comfortable?
Are you interested in fashion? Why/Why not?
Were you interested in clothes when you were a child?
What are your favourite clothes like now?

PART 2

Tip strip

- Choose a series that you can say a lot about, even if it's not the one you enjoy the most.
- Make notes about every bullet point, and about the line at the bottom (explain …).

Follow-up questions

You can just give a brief answer to follow-up questions.

You have one minute to make notes on the following topic. Then you have up to two minutes to talk about it.

Describe a TV series which you enjoy watching

You should say:

      what the series is about

      who presents it/acts in it

      how often it is on

and explain why you enjoy watching the series so much.

Is this series popular with many other people you know?
Do you watch TV often?

PART 3

Tip strip

Foreign programmes …

- **Question 3** When the question is long, you can say 'Pardon', or 'Sorry – could you say that again'. You will not lose marks for this.

Children and TV …

Use appropriate phrases for expressing opinions.

Changes in the media …

- **Question 1** Talk about both advantages and disadvantages.
- **Question 3** Use the future tense in your answer, and phrases like 'It's likely that …', 'I expect …' or 'Probably …'.

Consider these questions, and then answer them.

Let's talk about foreign TV programmes.

What kind of foreign TV programmes are popular in your country?
What are the advantages of having foreign-made programmes on TV?
Some people think governments should control the number of foreign-made TV programmes being shown. Do you agree? Why?

Now let's talk about children and TV.

What do you think are the qualities of a good children's TV programme?
What are the educational benefits of children watching TV?
Many people think adults should influence what children watch. Do you agree? Why?

Now let's talk about changes in the media.

What do you think are the advantages and disadvantages of having TV broadcast 24 hours a day?
In what ways have advances in technology influenced the way people watch TV?
What changes do you think will occur in broadcast media in the next 20 years?

TEST 3

Listening module (approx 30 minutes + 10 minutes transfer time)

Questions 1–10

Complete the notes below.

Write **NO MORE THAN ONE WORD OR A NUMBER** for each answer.

Car for sale (Mini)

Example

Age of car: just under ..13.. years old

Colour: **1** ....

Mileage: **2** ....

Previous owner was a **3** ....

Current owner has used car mainly for **4** ....

Price: may accept offers from **5** £ ....

(Note: **6** .... not due for 5 months)

Condition: good (recently serviced)

Will need a new **7** .... soon

Minor problem with a **8** ....

Viewing

Agreed to view the car on **9** .... a.m.

Address:

238, **10** .... Road.

Questions 11–20

Questions 11–14

*Choose the correct letter, **A**, **B** or **C**.*

11 The Treloar Valley passenger ferry

   A usually starts services in April.

   B departs at the same time each day.

   C is the main means of transport for local villagers.

12 What does the speaker say about the river cruise?

   A It can be combined with a train journey.

   B It's unsuitable for people who have walking difficulties.

   C The return journey takes up to four hours.

13 What information is given about train services in the area?

   A Trains run non-stop between Calton and Plymouth.

   B One section of the rail track is raised.

   C Bookings can be made by telephone or the Internet.

14 The 'Rover' bus ticket

   A can be used for up to five journeys a day.

   B is valid for weekend travel only.

   C has recently gone down in price.

Questions 15–20

Label the map below.

*Write the correct letter, **A–H**, next to questions 15–20.*

15 Bus stop ....

16 Car park ....

17 Museum ....

18 Mill ....

19 Potter's studio ....

20 Café ....

Questions 21–30

Questions 21–24

Choose the correct letter, **A**, **B** or **C**.

Advice on writing a dissertation

21 What does Howard say about the experience of writing his dissertation?

    A It was difficult in unexpected ways.

    B It was more enjoyable than he'd anticipated.

    C It helped him understand previous course work.

22 What is Joanne most worried about?

    A Finding enough material.

    B Missing deadlines.

    C Writing too much.

23 What does Howard say was his main worry a year previously?

    A Forgetting what he'd read about.

    B Not understanding what he'd read.

    C Taking such a long time to read each book.

24 What motivated Howard to start writing his dissertation?

    A Talking to his tutor about his problems.

    B Seeing an inspirational TV show.

    C Reading a controversial journal article.

Questions 25–30

Questions 25–26

*Choose **TWO** letters, **A–E**.*

What **TWO** things does Howard advise Joanne to do in the first month of tutorials?

    A See her tutor every week.

    B Review all the module booklists.

    C Buy all the key books.

    D Write full references for everything she reads.

    E Write a draft of the first chapter.

Questions 27–28

*Choose **TWO** letters, **A–E**.*

What **TWO** things does Howard say about library provision?

    A Staff are particularly helpful to undergraduates.

    B Inter-library loans are very reliable.

    C Students can borrow extra books when writing a dissertation.

    D Staff recommend relevant old dissertations.

    E It's difficult to access electronic resources.

Questions 29–30

*Choose **TWO** letters, **A–E**.*

What **TWO** things does Joanne agree to discuss with her tutor?

    A The best ways to collaborate with other students.

    B Who to get help from during college vacations.

    C The best way to present the research.

    D Whether she can use web sources.

    E How to manage her study time.

Questions 31–40

Questions 31–40

Complete the flow chart below.

Write **NO MORE THAN TWO WORDS** for each answer.

Expertise in creative writing

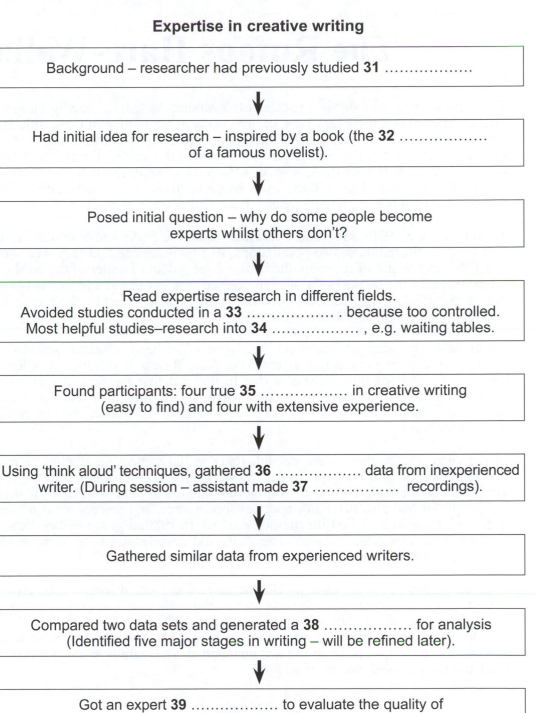

Background – researcher had previously studied **31** ....

↓

Had initial idea for research – inspired by a book (the **32** .... of a famous novelist).

↓

Posed initial question – why do some people become experts whilst others don't?

↓

Read expertise research in different fields.
Avoided studies conducted in a **33** .... because too controlled.
Most helpful studies–research into **34** .... , e.g. waiting tables.

↓

Found participants: four true **35** .... in creative writing (easy to find) and four with extensive experience.

↓

Using 'think aloud' techniques, gathered **36** .... data from inexperienced writer. (During session – assistant made **37** .... recordings).

↓

Gathered similar data from experienced writers.

↓

Compared two data sets and generated a **38** .... for analysis (Identified five major stages in writing – will be refined later).

↓

Got an expert **39** .... to evaluate the quality of the different products.

↓

Identified the most effective **40** .... of stages in producing text.

*You should spend about 20 minutes on **Questions 1–13**, which are based on Reading Passage 1 below.*

The Rufous Hare-Wallaby

The Rufous Hare-Wallaby is a species of Australian kangaroo, usually known by its Aboriginal name, 'mala'. At one time, there may have been as many as ten million of these little animals across the arid and semi-arid landscape of Australia, but their populations, like those of so many other small endemic species, were devastated when cats and foxes were introduced – indeed, during the 1950s it was thought that the mala was extinct. But in 1964, a small colony was found 450 miles northwest of Alice Springs in the Tanami Desert. And 12 years later, a second small colony was found nearby. Very extensive surveys were made throughout historical mala range – but no other traces were found.

Throughout the 1970s and 1980s, scientists from the Parks and Wildlife Commission of the Northern Territory monitored these two populations. At first it seemed that they were holding their own. Then in late 1987, every one of the individuals of the second and smaller of the wild colonies was killed. From examination of the tracks in the sand, it seemed that just one single fox had been responsible. And then, in October 1991, a wild-fire destroyed the entire area occupied by the remaining colony. Thus the mala was finally pronounced extinct in the wild.

Fortunately, ten years earlier, seven individuals had been captured, and had become the founders of a captive breeding programme at the Arid Zone Research Institute in Alice Springs; and that group had thrived. Part of this success is due to the fact that the female can breed when she is just five months old and can produce up to three young a year. Like other kangaroo species, the mother carries her young – known as a joey – in her pouch for about 15 weeks, and she can have more than one joey at the same time.

In the early 1980s, there were enough mala in the captive population to make it feasible to start a reintroduction programme. But first it was necessary to discuss this with the leaders of the Yapa people. Traditionally, the mala had been an important animal in their culture, with strong medicinal powers for old people. It had also been an important food source, and there were concerns that any mala returned to the wild would be killed for the pot. And so, in 1980, a group of key Yapa men was invited to visit the proposed reintroduction area. The skills and knowledge of the Yapa would play a significant and enduring role in this and all other mala projects.

With the help of the local Yapa, an electric fence was erected around 250 acres of suitable habitat, about 300 miles northwest of Alice Springs so that the mala could adapt while protected from predators. By 1992, there were about 150 mala in their enclosure, which became known as the Mala Paddock. However, all attempts to reintroduce mala from the paddocks into the unfenced wild were unsuccessful, so in the end the reintroduction programme was abandoned. The team now faced a situation where mala could be bred, but not released into the wild again.

Thus, in 1993, a Mala Recovery Team was established to boost mala numbers, and goals for a new programme were set: the team concentrated on finding suitable predator-free or predator-controlled conservation sites within the mala's known range. Finally, in March 1999, twelve adult females, eight adult males, and eight joeys were transferred from the Mala Paddock to Dryandra Woodland in Western Australia. Then, a few months later, a second group was transferred to Trimouille, an island off the coast of western Australia. First, it had been necessary to rid the island of rats and cats – a task that had taken two years of hard work.

Six weeks after their release into this conservation site, a team returned to the island to find out how things were going. Each of the malas had been fitted with a radio collar that transmits for about 14 months, after which it falls off. The team was able to locate 29 out of the 30 transmitters – only one came from the collar of a mala that had died of unknown causes. So far the recovery programme had gone even better than expected.

Today, there are many signs suggesting that the mala population on the island is continuing to do well.

Questions 1–5

Complete the flow chart below.

Choose **NO MORE THAN THREE WORDS AND/OR A NUMBER** *from the passage for each answer.*

The Wild Australian mala

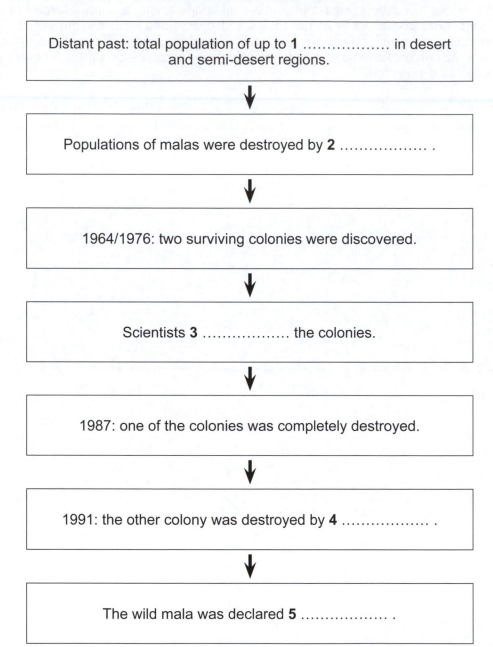

Distant past: total population of up to **1** .... in desert and semi-desert regions.

↓

Populations of malas were destroyed by **2** ....

↓

1964/1976: two surviving colonies were discovered.

↓

Scientists **3** .... the colonies.

↓

1987: one of the colonies was completely destroyed.

↓

1991: the other colony was destroyed by **4** ....

↓

The wild mala was declared **5** ....

Questions 6–9

Answer the questions below.

*Choose **NO MORE THAN THREE WORDS AND/OR A NUMBER** from the passage for each answer.*

6 At what age can female *malas* start breeding?

7 For about how long do young *malas* stay inside their mother's pouch?

8 Apart from being a food source, what value did *malas* have for the Yapa people?

9 What was the Yapa's lasting contribution to the *mala* reintroduction programme?

Questions 10–13

Do the following statements agree with the information given in Reading Passage 1?

Write

TRUE	*if the statement agrees with the information*
FALSE	*if the statement contradicts the information*
NOT GIVEN	*if there is no information on this*

10 Natural defences were sufficient to protect the area called Mala Paddock.

11 Scientists eventually gave up their efforts to release captive *mala* into the unprotected wild.

12 The *mala* population which was transferred to Dryandra Woodland quickly increased in size.

13 Scientists were satisfied with the initial results of the recovery programme.

You should spend about 20 minutes on **Questions 14–26**, which are based on Reading Passage 2 below.

Questions 14–26

Questions 14–19

Reading Passage 2 has **SEVEN** sections, **A–G**.

Choose the correct heading for sections **A–F** from the list of headings below.

Write the correct number, **i–viii**.

List of Headings

i	Outbreaks of plague as a result of military campaigns.
ii	Systematic intelligence-gathering about external cases of plague.
iii	Early forms of treatment for plague victims.
iv	The general limitations of early Russian anti-plague measures.
v	Partly successful bans against foreign states affected by plague.
vi	Hostile reactions from foreign states to Russian anti-plague measures.
vii	Various measures to limit outbreaks of plague associated with war.
viii	The formulation and publication of preventive strategies.

---

14 Section **A**   ....

15 Section **B**   ....

16 Section **C**   ....

17 Section **D**   ....

18 Section **E**   ....

19 Section **F**   ....

Measures to combat infectious disease in tsarist Russia

A In the second half of the seventeenth century, Russian authorities began implementing controls at the borders of their empire to prevent the importation of plague, a highly infectious and dangerous disease. Information on disease outbreak occurring abroad was regularly reported to the tsar's court through various means, including commercial channels (travelling merchants), military personnel deployed abroad, undercover agents, the network of Imperial Foreign Office embassies and representations abroad, and the customs offices. For instance, the heads of customs offices were instructed to question foreigners entering Russia about possible epidemics of dangerous diseases in their respective countries.

B If news of an outbreak came from abroad, relations with the affected country were suspended. For instance, foreign vessels were not allowed to dock in Russian ports if there was credible information about the existence of epidemics in countries from whence they had departed. In addition, all foreigners entering Russia from those countries had to undergo quarantine. In 1665, after receiving news about a plague epidemic in England, Tsar Alexei wrote a letter to King Charles II in which he announced the cessation of Russian trade relations with England and other foreign states. These protective measures appeared to have been effective, as the country did not record any cases of plague during that year and in the next three decades. It was not until 1692 that another plague outbreak was recorded in the Russian province of Astrakhan. This epidemic continued for five months and killed 10,383 people, or about 65 percent of the city's population. By the end of the seventeenth century, preventative measures had been widely introduced in Russia, including the isolation of persons ill with plague, the imposition of quarantines, and the distribution of explanatory public health notices about plague outbreaks.

C During the eighteenth century, although none of the occurrences was of the same scale as in the past, plague appeared in Russia several times. For instance, from 1703 to 1705, a plague outbreak that had ravaged Istanbul spread to the Podolsk and Kiev provinces in Russia, and then to Poland and Hungary. After defeating the Swedes in the battle of Poltava in 1709, Tsar Peter I (Peter the Great) dispatched part of his army to Poland, where plague had been raging for two years. Despite preventive measures, the disease spread among the Russian troops. In 1710, the plague reached Riga (then part of Sweden, now the capital of Latvia), where it was active until 1711 and claimed 60,000 lives. During this period, the Russians besieged Riga and, after the Swedes had surrendered the city in 1710, the Russian army lost 9,800 soldiers to the plague. Russian military chronicles of the time note that more soldiers died of the disease after the capture of Riga than from enemy fire during the siege of that city.

D Tsar Peter I imposed strict measures to prevent the spread of plague during these conflicts. Soldiers suspected of being infected were isolated and taken to areas far from military camps. In addition, camps were designed to separate divisions, detachments, and smaller units of soldiers. When plague reached Narva (located in present-day Estonia) and threatened to spread to St. Petersburg, the newly built capital of Russia, Tsar Peter I ordered the army to cordon off the entire boundary along the Luga River, including temporarily halting all activity on the river. In order to prevent the movement of people and goods from Narva to St Petersburg and Novgorod, roadblocks and checkpoints were set up on all roads. The tsar's orders were rigorously enforced, and those who disobeyed were hung.

E However, although the Russian authorities applied such methods to contain the spread of the disease and limit the number of victims, all of the measures had a provisional character: they were intended to respond to a specific outbreak, and were not designed as a coherent set of measures to be implemented systematically at the first sign of plague. The advent of such a standard response system came a few years later.

F The first attempts to organise procedures and carry out proactive steps to control plague date to the aftermath of the 1727-1728 epidemic in Astrakhan. In response to this, the Russian imperial authorities issued several decrees aimed at controlling the future spread of plague. Among these decrees, the 'Instructions for Governors and Heads of Townships' required that all governors immediately inform the Senate – a government body created by Tsar Peter I in 1711 to advise the monarch – if plague cases were detected in their respective provinces.

Furthermore, the decree required that governors ensure the physical examination of all persons suspected of carrying the disease and their subsequent isolation. In addition, it was ordered that sites where plague victims were found had to be encircled by checkpoints and isolated for the duration of the outbreak. These checkpoints were to remain operational for at least six weeks. The houses of infected persons were to be burned along with all of the personal property they contained, including farm animals and cattle. The governors were instructed to inform the neighbouring provinces and cities about every plague case occurring on their territories. Finally, letters brought by couriers were heated above a fire before being copied.

G The implementation by the authorities of these combined measures demonstrates their intuitive understanding of the importance of the timely isolation of infected people to limit the spread of plague.

Questions 20–21

*Choose **TWO** letters, **A–E**.*

Write the correct letters.

Which **TWO** measures did Russia take in the seventeenth century to avoid plague outbreaks?

    A Cooperation with foreign leaders.

    B Spying.

    C Military campaigns.

    D Restrictions on access to its ports.

    E Expulsion of foreigners.

Questions 22–23

*Choose **TWO** letters, **A–E**.*

Write the correct letters.

Which **TWO** statements are made about Russia in the early eighteenth century?

    A Plague outbreaks were consistently smaller than before.

    B Military casualties at Riga exceeded the number of plague victims.

    C The design of military camps allowed plague to spread quickly.

    D The tsar's plan to protect St Petersburg from plague was not strictly implemented.

    E Anti-plague measures were generally reactive rather than strategic.

Questions 24–26

Complete the sentences below.

*Choose **ONE WORD ONLY** from the passage for each answer.*

24 An outbreak of plague in ……………… prompted the publication of a coherent preventative strategy.

25 Provincial governors were ordered to burn the ……………… and possessions of plague victims.

26 Correspondence was held over a ……………… prior to copying it.

Recovering a damaged reputation

In 2009, it was revealed that some of the information published by the University of East Anglia's Climatic Research Unit (CRU) in the UK, concerning climate change, had been inaccurate. Furthermore, it was alleged that some of the relevant statistics had been withheld from publication. The ensuing controversy affected the reputation not only of that institution, but also of the Intergovernmental Panel on Climate Change (IPCC), with which the CRU is closely involved, and of climate scientists in general. Even if the claims of misconduct and incompetence were eventually proven to be largely untrue, or confined to a few individuals, the damage was done. The perceived wrongdoings of a few people had raised doubts about the many.

The response of most climate scientists was to cross their fingers and hope for the best, and they kept a low profile. Many no doubt hoped that subsequent independent inquiries into the IPCC and CRU would draw a line under their problems. However, although these were likely to help, they were unlikely to undo the harm caused by months of hostile news reports and attacks by critics.

The damage that has been done should not be underestimated. As Ralph Cicerone, the President of the US National Academy of Sciences, wrote in an editorial in the journal *Science*: 'Public opinion has moved toward the view that scientists often try to suppress alternative hypotheses and ideas and that scientists will withhold data and try to manipulate some aspects of peer review to prevent dissent.' He concluded that 'the perceived misbehavior of even a few scientists can diminish the credibility of science as a whole.'

An opinion poll taken at the beginning of 2010 found that the proportion of people in the US who trust scientists as a source of information about global warming had dropped from 83 percent, in 2008, to 74 percent. Another survey carried out by the British Broadcasting Corporation in February 2010 found that just 26 percent of British people now believe that climate change is confirmed as being largely human-made, down from 41 percent in November 2009.

Regaining the confidence and trust of the public is never easy. Hunkering down and hoping for the best – climate science's current strategy – makes it almost impossible. It is much better to learn from the successes and failures of organisations that have dealt with similar blows to their public standing.

In fact, climate science needs professional help to rebuild its reputation. It could do worse than follow the advice given by Leslie Gaines-Ross, a 'reputation strategist' at Public Relations (PR) company Weber Shandwick, in her recent book *Corporate Reputation: 12 Steps to Safeguarding and Recovering Reputation*. Gaines-Ross's strategy is based on her analysis of how various organisations responded to crises, such as desktop-printer firm Xerox, whose business plummeted during the 1990s, and the USA's National Aeronautics and Space Administration (NASA) after the Columbia shuttle disaster in 2003.

The first step she suggests is to 'take the heat – leader first'. In many cases, chief executives who publicly accept responsibility for corporate failings can begin to reverse the freefall of their company's reputations, but not always. If the leader is held at least partly responsible for the fall from grace, it can be almost impossible to convince critics that a new direction can be charted with that same person at the helm.

This is the dilemma facing the heads of the IPCC and CRU. Both have been blamed for their organisations' problems, not least for the way in which they have dealt with critics, and both have been subjected to public calls for their removal. Yet both organisations appear to believe they can repair their reputations without a change of leadership.

The second step outlined by Gaines-Ross is to 'communicate tirelessly'. Yet many climate researchers have avoided the media and the public, at least until the official enquiries have concluded their reports. This reaction may be understandable, but it has backfired. Journalists following the story have often been unable to find spokespeople willing to defend climate science. In this case, 'no comment' is commonly interpreted as an admission of silent, collective guilt.

Remaining visible is only a start, though; climate scientists also need to be careful what they say. They must realise that they face doubts not just about their published results, but also about their conduct and honesty. It simply won't work for scientists to continue to appeal to the weight of the evidence, while refusing to discuss the integrity of their profession. The harm has been increased by a perceived reluctance to admit even the possibility of mistakes or wrongdoing.

The third step put forward by Gaines-Ross is 'don't underestimate your critics and competitors'. This means not only recognising the skill with which the opponents of climate research have executed their campaigns through Internet blogs and other media, but also acknowledging the validity of some of their criticisms. It is clear, for instance, that climate scientists need better standards of transparency, to allow for scrutiny not just by their peers, but also by critics from outside the world of research.

It is also important to engage with those critics. That doesn't mean conceding to unfounded arguments which are based on prejudice rather than evidence, but there is an obligation to help the public understand the causes of climate change, as well as the options for avoiding and dealing with the consequences.

To begin the process of rebuilding trust in their profession, climate scientists need to follow these three steps. But that is just the start. Gaines-Ross estimates that it typically takes four years for a company to rescue and restore a broken reputation.

Winning back public confidence is a marathon, not a sprint, but you can't win at all if you don't step up to the starting line.

Questions 27–40

Questions 27–32

Do the following statements agree with the views of the writer in Reading Passage 3?

Write

YES if the statement agrees with the claims of the writer
NO if the statement contradicts the claims of the writer
NOT GIVEN if it is impossible to say what the writer thinks about this

27 If a majority of scientists at the CRU were cleared of misconduct, the public would be satisfied.

28 In the aftermath of the CRU scandal, most scientists avoided attention.

29 Journalists have defended the CRU and the IPCC against their critics.

30 Ralph Cicerone regarded the damage caused by the CRU as extending beyond the field of climate science.

31 Since 2010, confidence in climate science has risen slightly in the US.

32 Climate scientists should take professional advice on regaining public confidence.

Questions 33–36

Choose the correct letter, **A, B, C** or **D**.

33 In accordance with Gaines-Ross's views, the heads of the CRU and IPCC should have

   A resigned from their posts.

   B accepted responsibility and continued in their posts.

   C shifted attention onto more junior staff.

   D ignored the criticisms directed at them.

34 Which mistake have staff at the CRU and IPCC made?

   A They have blamed each other for problems.

   B They have publicly acknowledged failings.

   C They have avoided interviews with the press.

   D They have made conflicting public statements.

35 People who challenge the evidence of climate change have generally

   A presented their case poorly.

   B missed opportunities for publicity.

   C made some criticisms which are justified.

   D been dishonest in their statements.

36 What does the reference to 'a marathon' indicate in the final paragraph?

    A The rate at which the climate is changing.

    B The competition between rival theories of climate change.

    C The ongoing need for new climate data.

    D The time it might take for scientists to win back confidence.

Questions 37–40

*Complete the summary using the list of words/phrases, **A–H**, below.*

Controversy about climate science

The revelation, in 2009, that scientists at the CRU had presented inaccurate information and concealed some of their **37**....had a serious effect on their reputation. In order to address the problem, the scientists should turn to experts in **38**....

Leslie Gaines-Ross has published **39**....based on studies of crisis management in commercial and public-sector organisations. Amongst other things, Gaines-Ross suggests that climate scientists should confront their **40**.....

A critics	**B** corruption	**C** statistics	**D** guidelines
E managers	**F** public relations	**G** sources	**H** computer modelling

Writing module (1 hour)

You should spend about 20 minutes on this task.

> **The bar chart below shows the percentage of unemployed graduates, aged 20-24, in one European country over a two-year period.**
>
> **Summarise the information by selecting and reporting the main features, and making comparisons where relevant.**

Write at least 150 words.

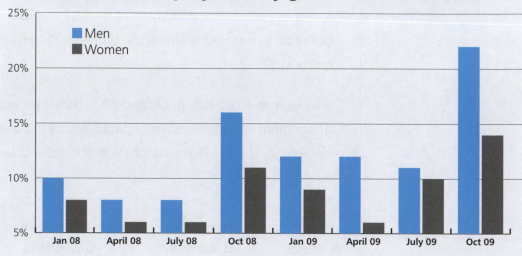

Graduate unemployment by gender, 2008 and 2009

You should spend about 40 minutes on this task.

Write about the following topic:

> **Many people assume that the goal of every country should be to produce more materials and goods.**
>
> **To what extent do you agree or disagree that constantly increasing production is an appropriate goal?**

Give reasons for your answer, and include any relevant examples from your own knowledge or experience.

Write at least 250 words.

Speaking module (11–14 minutes)

PART 1   Answer these questions.

Let's talk about what you do.

Do you work, or are you a student?
EITHER
What subjects do you study?
Why did you choose this course?
OR
What's your job?
Why did you choose this job?

Now let's talk about reading.

Did your parents read to you when you were a child? Why/Why not?
Do you read for pleasure very often? Why/Why not?
What kind of books or magazines do you buy? Why/Why not?
Which do you find easier, reading in English or writing in English? Why?

PART 2   You have one minute to make notes on the following topic. Then you have up to two minutes to talk about it.

> Describe an elderly person in your family who you enjoy talking to.
>
> You should say:
>
> > who the person is
> >
> > what he/she is like
> >
> > how often you see him/her
>
> and explain why you enjoy talking to this person.

Do other people in your family like talking to this person too?
When did you last see this person?

PART 3   Consider these questions, and then answer them.

Let's go on to talk about elderly people who live with their families.

In your country, do most grandparents live in the same house as their children and grandchildren? Why/Why not?
What are the advantages and disadvantages for grandparents of living in the same house as their children and grandchildren?

Now let's talk about retirement.

Do you think some people retire from their jobs too early? Why/Why not?
Why do you think some people feel unhappy when they first retire from work?
What types of hobby do people enjoy doing after they have retired from work?

Now let's consider old age in the future.

What kinds of problem can be caused when the proportion of elderly people in a country keeps rising?
In what ways might the lives of elderly people be different in the future? Why/Why not?

TEST 4

Listening module (approx 30 minutes + 10 minutes transfer time)

Questions 1–10

Complete the notes below.

Write **ONE WORD AND/OR A NUMBER** for each answer.

Things to do before we go

Example

- Collect the <u>currency</u>.

- Cancel appointment with the **1** .... (Monday)

- Begin taking the **2** .... (Tuesday)

- Buy

  3 .... ,

  a small bag,

  a spare **4** .... ,

  an electrical **5** ....

- Book a **6** ....

Instructions for Laura's mum

- Feed the cat

Vet's details:

Name: Colin **7** ....

Tel: **8** ....

Address: Fore Street (opposite the **9** ....)

- Water the plants

- Meet the heating engineer on **10** ....

Questions 11–20

Questions 11–16

Choose the correct answer, **A**, **B** or **C**.

Adbourne Film Festival

11 Why was the Film Festival started?

    A To encourage local people to make films.

    B To bring more tourists to the town.

    C To use money released from another project.

12 What is the price range for tickets?

    A £1.00 – £2.50

    B 50p – £2.00

    C £1.50 – £2.50

13 As well as online, tickets for the films can be obtained

    A from the local library.

    B from several different shops.

    C from the two festival cinemas.

14 Last year's winning film was about

    A farms of the future.

    B schools and the environment.

    C green transport options.

15 This year the competition prize is

    A a stay in a hotel.

    B film-making equipment.

    C a sum of money.

16 The deadline for entering a film in the competition is the end of

    A May.

    B June.

    C July.

Questions 17–20

Questions 17–18

*Choose **TWO** letters, **A–E**.*

What **TWO** main criteria are used to judge the film competition?

    A Ability to persuade.

    B Quality of the story.

    C Memorable characters.

    D Quality of photography.

    E Originality.

Questions 19–20

*Choose **TWO** letters, **A–E**.*

What **TWO** changes will be made to the competition next year?

    A A new way of judging.

    B A different length of film.

    C An additional age category.

    D Different performance times.

    E New locations for performances.

Questions 21–30

Questions 21–24

*Choose the correct letter, **A**, **B** or **C**.*

Research on web-based crosswords

21 Leela and Jake chose this article because

    A it was on a topic familiar to most students.

    B it covered both IT and education issues.

    C it dealt with a very straightforward concept.

22 How did Leela and Jake persuade students to take part in their research?

    A They convinced them they would enjoy the experience.

    B They said it would help them do a particular test.

    C They offered to help them with their own research later on.

23 Leela and Jake changed the design of the original questionnaire because

    A it was too short for their purposes.

    B it asked misleading questions.

    C it contained out-of-date points.

24 Leela was surprised by the fact that

    A it is normal for questionnaire returns to be low.

    B so many students sent back their questionnaires.

    C the questionnaire responses were of such high quality.

Questions 25–30

Questions 25–26

*Choose **TWO** letters, **A–E**.*

What **TWO** things did respondents say they liked most about doing the crossword?

    A It helped them spell complex technical terms.

    B It was an enjoyable experience.

    C It helped them concentrate effectively.

    D It increased their general motivation to study.

    E It showed what they still needed to study.

Questions 27–28

*Choose **TWO** letters, **A–E**.*

In which **TWO** areas did these research findings differ from those of the original study?

    A Students' interest in doing similar exercises.

    B How much students liked doing the crossword.

    C Time taken to do the crossword.

    D Gender differences in appreciation.

    E Opinions about using crosswords for formal assessment.

Questions 29–30

*Choose **TWO** letters, **A–E**.*

What **TWO** skills did Leela and Jake agree they had learned from doing the project?

    A How to manage their time effectively.

    B How to process numerical data.

    C How to design research tools.

    D How to reference other people's work.

    E How to collaborate in research.

Questions 31–40

Complete the sentences below.

Write **NO MORE THAN TWO WORDS** *for each answer.*

Job satisfaction study

31 Workers involved in the study were employed at a ……………… .

32 Despite some apparent differences between groups of workers, the survey results were statistically ……………… .

33 The speaker analysed the study's ……………… to identify any problems with it.

34 The various sub-groups were …………………… in size.

35 Workers in the part-time group were mainly ……………… .

36 The ……………… of workers who agreed to take part in the study was disappointing.

37 Researchers were unable to ……………… the circumstances in which workers filled out the questionnaire.

38 In future, the overall size of the ……………… should be increased.

39 In future studies, workers should be prevented from having discussions with ……………… .

40 Workers should be reassured that their responses to questions are ……………… .

You should spend about 20 minutes on **Questions 1–13**, which are based on Reading Passage 1 below.

Geoff Brash

Geoff Brash, who died in 2010, was a gregarious Australian businessman and philanthropist who encouraged the young to reach their potential.

Born in Melbourne to Elsa and Alfred Brash, he was educated at Scotch College. His sister, Barbara, became a renowned artist and printmaker. His father, Alfred, ran the Brash retail music business that had been founded in 1862 by his grandfather, the German immigrant Marcus Brasch, specialising in pianos. It carried the slogan 'A home is not a home without a piano.'

In his young days, Brash enjoyed the good life, playing golf and sailing, and spending some months travelling through Europe, having a leisurely holiday. He worked for a time at Myer department stores before joining the family business in 1949, where he quickly began to put his stamp on things. In one of his first management decisions, he diverged from his father's sense of frugal aesthetics by re-carpeting the old man's office while he was away. After initially complaining of his extravagance, his father grew to accept the change and gave his son increasing responsibility in the business.

After World War II (1939–1945), Brash's had begun to focus on white goods, such as washing machines and refrigerators, as the consumer boom took hold. However, while his father was content with the business he had built, the younger Brash viewed expansion as vital. When Geoff Brash took over as managing director in 1957, the company had two stores, but after floating it on the stock exchange the following year, he expanded rapidly and opened suburban stores, as well as buying into familiar music industry names such as Allans, Palings and Suttons. Eventually, 170 stores traded across the continent under the Brash's banner.

Geoff Brash learned from his father's focus on customer service. Alfred Brash had also been a pioneer in introducing a share scheme for his staff, and his son retained and expanded the plan following the float.

Geoff Brash was optimistic and outward looking. As a result, he was a pioneer in both accessing and selling new technology, and developing overseas relationships. He sourced and sold electric guitars, organs, and a range of other modern instruments, as well as state-of-the-art audio and video equipment. He developed a relationship with Taro Kakehashi, the founder of Japan's Roland group, which led to a joint venture that brought electronic musical devices to Australia.

In 1965, Brash and his wife attended a trade fair in Guangzhou, the first of its kind in China; they were one of the first Western business people allowed into the country following Mao Zedong's Cultural Revolution. He returned there many times, helping advise the Chinese in establishing a high quality piano factory in Beijing; he became the factory's agent in Australia. Brash also took leading jazz musicians Don Burrows and James Morrison to China, on a trip that reintroduced jazz to many Chinese musicians.

He stood down as Executive Chairman of Brash's in 1988, but under the new management debt became a problem, and in 1994 the banks called in administrators. The company was sold to Singaporean interests and continued to trade until 1998, when it again went into administration. The Brash name then disappeared from the retail world. Brash was greatly disappointed by the collapse and the eventual disappearance of the company he had run for so long. But it was not long before he invested in a restructured Allan's music business.

Brash was a committed philanthropist who, in the mid-1980s, established the Brash Foundation, which eventually morphed, with other partners, into the Soundhouse Music Alliance. This was a not-for-profit organisation overseeing and promoting multimedia music making and education for teachers and students. The Soundhouse offers teachers and young people the opportunity to get exposure to the latest music technology, and to use this to compose and record their own music, either alone or in collaboration. The organisation has now also established branches in New Zealand, South Africa and Ireland, as well as numerous sites around Australia.

Questions 1–13

Questions 1–5

Do the following statements agree with the information given in Reading Passage 1?

Write

TRUE	*if the statement agrees with the information*
FALSE	*if the statement contradicts the information*
NOT GIVEN	*if there is no information on this*

1   The Brash business originally sold pianos.

2   Geoff Brash's first job was with his grandfather's company.

3   Alfred Brash thought that his son wasted money.

4   By the time Geoff Brash took control, the Brash business was selling some electrical products.

5   Geoff Brash had ambitions to open Brash stores in other countries.

Questions 6–10

Answer the questions below.

Choose **NO MORE THAN THREE WORDS OR A NUMBER** *from the passage for each answer.*

6   Which arrangement did Alfred Brash set up for his employees?

7   Which Japanese company did Geoff Brash collaborate with?

8   What type of event in China marked the beginning of Geoff Brash's relationship with that country?

9   What style of music did Geoff Brash help to promote in China?

10 When did the Brash company finally stop doing business?

Questions 11–13

Complete the notes below.

*Choose **ONE WORD ONLY** from the passage for each answer.*

Soundhouse Music Alliance

- Grew out of the Brash Foundation.

- A non-commercial organisation providing support for music and music **11** ....

- Allows opportunities for using up-to-date **12** ....

- Has **13** .... in several countries.

You should spend about 20 minutes on **Questions 14–26**, which are based on Reading Passage 2 below.

Questions 14–26

Questions 14–19

Reading Passage 2 has **SIX** paragraphs, **A–F**.

Choose the correct heading, **A–F**, from the list of headings below.

Write the correct number, **i–ix**.

List of Headings

i	A mixture of languages and nationalities
ii	The creation of an exclusive identity
iii	The duties involved in various occupations
iv	An unprecedented population density
v	Imports and exports transported by river
vi	Transporting heavy loads manually
vii	Temporary work for large numbers of people
viii	Hazards associated with riverside work
ix	The changing status of riverside occupations

---

14 Paragraph **A**   ....

15 Paragraph **B**   ....

16 Paragraph **C**   ....

17 Paragraph **D**   ....

18 Paragraph **E**   ....

19 Paragraph **F**   ....

Early occupations around the river Thames

A In her pioneering survey, *Sources of London English*, Laura Wright has listed the variety of medieval workers who took their livings from the river Thames. The *baillies* of Queenhithe and Billingsgate acted as customs officers. There were *conservators*, who were responsible for maintaining the embankments and the weirs, and there were the *garthmen* who worked in the fish garths (enclosures). Then there were *galleymen* and *lightermen* and *shoutmen*, called after the names of their boats, and there were *hookers* who were named after the manner in which they caught their fish. The *searcher* patrolled the Thames in search of illegal fish weirs, and the *tideman* worked on its banks and foreshores whenever the tide permitted him to do so.

B All of these occupations persisted for many centuries, as did those jobs that depended upon the trade of the river. Yet, it was not easy work for any of the workers. They carried most goods upon their backs, since the rough surfaces of the quays and nearby streets were not suitable for wagons or large carts; the merchandise characteristically arrived in barrels which could be rolled from the ship along each quay. If the burden was too great to be carried by a single man, then the goods were slung on poles resting on the shoulders of two men. It was a slow and expensive method of business.

C However, up to the eighteenth century, river work was seen in a generally favourable light. For Langland, writing in the fourteenth century, the labourers working on river merchandise were relatively prosperous. And the porters of the seventeenth and early eighteenth centuries were, if anything, aristocrats of labour, enjoying high status. However, in the years from the late eighteenth to the early nineteenth century, there was a marked change in attitude. This was in part because the working river was within the region of the East End of London, which in this period acquired an unenviable reputation. By now, dockside labour was considered to be the most disreputable, and certainly the least desirable form of work.

D It could be said that the first industrial community in England grew up around the Thames. With the host of river workers themselves, as well as the vast assembly of ancillary trades such as tavern-keepers and laundresses, food-sellers and street-hawkers, shopkeepers and marine store dealers – there was a workforce of many thousands congregated in a relatively small area. There were more varieties of business to be observed by the riverside than in any other part of the city. As a result, with the possible exception of the area known as Seven Dials, the East End was also the most intensively inhabited region of London.

E It was a world apart, with its own language and its own laws. From the sailors in the opium dens of Limehouse to the smugglers on the malarial flats of the estuary, the workers of the river were not part of any civilised society. The alien world of the river had entered them. That alienation was also expressed in the slang of the docks, which essentially amounted to backslang, or the reversal of ordinary words. This backslang also helped in the formulation of Cockney rhyming slang*, so that the vocabulary of Londoners was directly affected by the life of the Thames.

F The reports in the nineteenth-century press reveal a heterogeneous world of dock labour, in which the crowds of casuals waiting for work at the dock gates at 7.45 a.m. include penniless refugees, bankrupts, old soldiers, broken-down gentlemen, discharged servants, and ex-convicts. There were some 400-500 permanent workers who earned a regular wage and who were considered to be the patricians of dockside labour. However, there were some 2,500 casual workers who were hired by the shift. The work for which they competed fiercely had become ever more unpleasant. Steam power could not be used for the cranes, for example, because of the danger of fire. So the cranes were powered by treadmills. Six to eight men entered a wooden cylinder and, laying hold of ropes, would tread the wheel round. They could lift nearly 20 tonnes to an average height of 27 feet (8.2 metres), forty times in an hour. This was part of the life of the river unknown to those who were intent upon its more picturesque aspects.

---

* a collection of phrases, based on rhyme, used by people in parts of central London as alternatives to standard English words.

Questions 20–21

*Choose **TWO** letters, **A–E**.*

Write the correct letters.

Which **TWO** statements are made about work by the River Thames before the eighteenth century?

    A   Goods were transported from the river by cart.

    B   The workforce was very poorly paid.

    C   Occupations were specialised.

    D   Workers were generally looked down upon.

    E   Physical strength was required.

Questions 22–23

*Choose **TWO** letters, **A–E**.*

Write the correct letters.

Which **TWO** statements are made about life by the River Thames in the early nineteenth century?

    A   The area was very crowded.

    B   There was an absence of crime.

    C   Casual work was in great demand.

    D   Several different languages were in use.

    E   Inhabitants were known for their friendliness.

Questions 24–26

Complete the sentences below.

*Use **NO MORE THAN TWO WORDS** from the passage for each answer.*

24 In the nineteenth century, only a minority of dock workers received
a ....

25 Cranes were operated manually because .... created a risk of fire.

26 Observers who were unfamiliar with London's docks found the River
Thames ....

Video game research

Although video games were first developed for adults, they are no longer exclusively reserved for the grown ups in the home. In 2006, Rideout and Hamel reported that as many as 29 percent of preschool children (children between two and six years old) in the United States had played console video games, and 18 percent had played hand-held ones. Given young children's insatiable eagerness to learn, coupled with the fact that they are clearly surrounded by these media, we predict that preschoolers will both continue and increasingly begin to adopt video games for personal enjoyment. Although the majority of gaming equipment is still designed for a much older target audience, once a game system enters the household it is potentially available for all family members, including the youngest. Portable systems have done a particularly good job of penetrating the younger market.

Research in the video game market is typically done at two stages: some time close to the end of the product cycle, in order to get feedback from consumers, so that a marketing strategy can be developed; and at the very end of the product cycle to 'fix bugs' in the game. While both of those types of research are important, and may be appropriate for dealing with adult consumers, neither of them aids in designing better games, especially when it comes to designing for an audience that may have particular needs, such as preschoolers or senior citizens. Instead, exploratory and formative research has to be undertaken in order to truly understand those audiences, their abilities, their perspective, and their needs. In the spring of 2007, our preschool-game production team at Nickelodeon had a hunch that the *Nintendo DS*[*] – with its new features, such as the microphone, small size and portability, and its relatively low price point – was a ripe gaming platform for preschoolers. There were a few games on the market at the time which had characters that appealed to the younger set, but our game producers did not think that the game mechanics or design were appropriate for preschoolers. What exactly preschoolers *could* do with the system, however, was a bit of a mystery. So we set about doing a study to answer the query: What could we expect preschoolers to be capable of in the context of hand-held game play, and how might the child development literature inform us as we proceeded with the creation of a new outlet for this age group?

Our context in this case was the United States, although the games that resulted were also released in other regions, due to the broad international reach of the characters. In order to design the best possible DS product for a preschool audience we were fully committed to the ideals of a 'user-centered approach', which assumes that users will be at least considered, but ideally consulted during the development process. After all, when it comes to introducing a new interactive product to the child market, and particularly such a young age group within it, we believe it is crucial to assess the range of physical and cognitive abilities associated with their specific developmental stage.

Revelle and Medoff (2002) review some of the basic reasons why home entertainment systems, computers, and other electronic gaming devices, are often difficult for preschoolers to use. In addition to their still developing motor skills (which make manipulating a controller with small buttons difficult), many of the major stumbling blocks are cognitive. Though preschoolers are learning to think symbolically, and understand that pictures can stand for real-life objects, the vast majority are still unable to read and write. Thus, using text-based menu selections is not viable. Mapping is yet another obstacle since preschoolers may be unable to understand that there is a direct link between how the controller is used and the activities that appear before them on screen. Though this aspect is changing, in traditional mapping systems real life movements do not usually translate into game-based activity.

Over the course of our study, we gained many insights into how preschoolers interact with various platforms, including the DS. For instance, all instructions for preschoolers need to be in voiceover, and include visual representations, and this has been one of the most difficult areas for us to negotiate with respect to game design on the DS. Because the game cartridges have very limited memory capacity, particularly in comparison to console or computer games, the ability to capture large amounts of voiceover data via sound files or visual representations of instructions becomes limited. Text instructions take up minimal memory, so they are preferable from a technological perspective. Figuring out ways to maximise sound and graphics files, while retaining the clear visual and verbal cues that we know are critical for our youngest players, is a constant give and take. Another of our findings indicated that preschoolers may use either a stylus, or their fingers, or both although they are not very accurate with either. One of the very interesting aspects of the DS is that the interface, which is designed to respond to stylus interactions, can also effectively be used with the tip of the finger. This is particularly noteworthy in the context of preschoolers for two reasons. Firstly, as they have trouble with fine motor skills and their hand-eye coordination is still in development, they are less exact with their stylus movements; and secondly, their fingers are so small that they mimic the stylus very effectively, and therefore by using their fingers they can often be more accurate in their game interactions.

---

* a brand of hand-held electronic games

Questions 27–40

Questions 27–31

Do the following statements agree with the claims of the writer in Reading Passage 3?

Write

YES　　　　*if the statement agrees with the claims of the writer*
NO　　　　*if the statement contradicts the claims of the writer*
NOT GIVEN　*if it is impossible to say what the writer thinks about this*

27　Video game use amongst preschool children is higher in the US than in other countries.

28　The proportion of preschool children using video games is likely to rise.

29　Parents in the US who own gaming equipment generally allow their children to play with it.

30　The type of research which manufacturers usually do is aimed at improving game design.

31　Both old and young games consumers require research which is specifically targeted.

Questions 32–36

Complete the summary using the list of words/phrases, A–I, below.

Problems for preschool users of video games

Preschool children find many electronic games difficult, because neither their motor skills nor their **32** ……………… are sufficiently developed.

Certain types of control are hard for these children to manipulate: for example, **33** ……………… can be more effective than styluses. Also, although they already have the ability to relate **34** ……………… to real-world objects, preschool children are largely unable to understand the connection between their own **35** ……………… and the movements they can see on the screen. Finally, very few preschool children can understand **36** ……………… .

A actions	**B** buttons	**C** cognitive skills
D concentration	**E** fingers	**F** pictures　　**G** sounds
H spoken instructions	**I** written menus	

Questions 37–40

*Choose the correct letter, **A**, **B**, **C** or **D**.*

37 In 2007, what conclusion did games producers at Nickelodeon come to?

    A The preschool market was unlikely to be sufficiently profitable.

    B One of their hardware products would probably be suitable for preschoolers.

    C Games produced by rival companies were completely inappropriate for preschoolers.

    D They should put their ideas for new games for preschoolers into practice.

38 The study carried out by Nickelodeon

    A was based on children living in various parts of the world.

    B focused on the kinds of game content which interests preschoolers.

    C investigated the specific characteristics of the target market.

    D led to products which appealed mainly to the US consumers.

39 Which problem do the writers highlight concerning games instructions for young children?

    A Spoken instructions take up a lot of the available memory.

    B Written instructions have to be expressed very simply.

    C The children do not follow instructions consistently.

    D The video images distract attention from the instructions.

40 Which is the best title for Reading Passage 3?

    A An overview of video games software for the preschool market

    B Researching and designing video games for preschool children

    C The effects of video games on the behaviour of young children

    D Assessing the impact of video games on educational achievement

Writing module (1 hour)

You should spend about 20 minutes on this task.

> **The charts below show the percentage of monthly household income spent on various items by two different groups in one European country.**
>
> **Summarise the information by selecting and reporting the main features, and make comparisons where relevant.**

Write at least 150 words.

Percentage of household income spent on different items*
Low income group

- Food and drink 29%
- Fuel bills 24%
- Miscellaneous 18%
- Recreation/culture 11%
- Transport 9%
- Clothing 5%
- Restaurant/hotels 4%

Percentage of household income spent on different items*
High income group

- Miscellaneous 23%
- Recreation/culture 21%
- Transport 16%
- Food and drink 15%
- Restaurant/hotels 12%
- Fuel bills 7%
- Clothing 6%

* Earnings excluding house rent/purchase

You should spend about 40 minutes on this task.

Write about the following topic:

> **Modern technology has made it easier for individuals to download copyrighted music and books from the internet for no charge.**
>
> **To what extent is this a positive or a negative development?**

Give reasons for your answer, and include any relevant examples from your own knowledge or experience.

Write at least 250 words.

Speaking module (11–14 minutes)

Answer these questions.

Let's talk about your country.

What is the area where you live like?
Have you always lived in the same part of the country? Why/Why not?
Do many visitors travel to your country?
What do visitors to your country like to see and do?

Now let's talk about food.

What is your favourite type of food? Why?
Do you prefer eating at home or in a restaurant? Why/Why not?
When was the first time you cooked something yourself? What?
How happy are you to try eating new things? Why?

PART 2 You have one minute to make notes on the following topic. Then you have up to two minutes to talk about it.

Describe a present that someone gave you which you liked a lot.

You should say:

what the present was

who gave it to you

why the person gave you a present

and explain why you liked that present a lot.

Were you surprised to receive that present?
Do you still have that present?

PART 3 Consider these questions and then answer them.

Now let's talk about giving presents in your country.

On which occasions do people in your country usually give presents?
How important is it to wrap presents in an attractive way? Why/Why not?
Do people who receive a present usually open it straight away, or do they open it later? Why/Why not?

Now let's talk about official charities (e.g. Oxfam, UNICEF).

How important is it for people to support and give aid to charities? Why/ Why not?
What do you think the role of official charities should be?
Why can charities sometimes help people more effectively than government organisations can?

Listening module (approx 30 minutes + 10 minutes transfer time)

Questions 1–10

Questions 1–2

Complete the notes below.

Write **NO MORE THAN ONE WORD** for each answer.

Advice on plumbers and decorators

Example
Make sure the company is : local.

Don't call a plumber during the **1** ....

Look at trade website: **2** www. .... .com

Questions 3–10

Complete the table below.

Write **NO MORE THAN ONE WORD** for each answer.

Name	Positive points	Negative points
Peake's Plumbing	• Pleasant and friendly • Give **3** .... information • Good quality work	• Always **4** ....
John Damerol Plumbing Services	• **5**. .... than other companies • Reliable	• Not very polite • Tends to be **6** ....
Simonson Plasterers	• Able to do lots of different **7**	• More **8** .... than other companies
H.L. Plastering	• Reliable. • Also able to do **9**	• Prefers not to use long **10** ....

Questions 11–20

Questions 11–15

Choose the correct answer, **A**, **B** or **C**.

Museum work placement

11 On Monday, what will be the students' working day?

    A 9.00 a.m. – 5.00 p.m.

    B 8.45 a.m. – 5.00 p.m.

    C 9.00 a.m. – 4.45 p.m.

12 While working in the museum, students are encouraged to wear

    A formal clothing such as a suit.

    B a cap with the museum logo.

    C their own casual clothes.

13 If students are ill or going to be late, they must inform

    A the museum receptionist.

    B their museum supervisor.

    C their school placement tutor.

14 The most popular task whilst on work placement is usually

    A making presentations in local primary schools.

    B talking to elderly people in care homes.

    C conducting workshops in the museum.

15 The best form of preparation before starting their work placement is to read

    A the history of the museum on the website.

    B the museum regulations and safety guidance.

    C notes made by previous work placement students.

Questions 16–20

Label the plan below.

*Write the correct letter, **A–I**, next to questions 16–20*

Where in the museum are the following places?

16 Sign-in office   ....

17 Gallery 1   ....

18 Key box   ....

19 Kitchen area   ....

20 Staff noticeboard   ....

Questions 21–30

Questions 21–26

What is the tutor's opinion of the following company projects?

*Choose **FIVE** answers from the box, and write the correct letter, **A–H**, next to questions 21–26.*

Tutor's opinion

A It would be very rewarding for the student.

B It is too ambitious.

C It would be difficult to evaluate.

D It wouldn't be sufficiently challenging.

E It would involve extra costs.

F It is beyond the student's current ability.

G It is already being done by another student.

H It would probably have the greatest impact on the company.

Company projects

21 Customer database ....

22 Online sales catalogue ....

23 Payroll ....

24 Stock inventory ....

25 Internal security ....

26 Customer services ....

Questions 27–30

Questions 27–28

*Choose **TWO** letters, **A–E**.*

Which **TWO** problems do Sam and the tutor identify concerning group assignments?

    A Personal relationships.

    B Cultural differences.

    C Division of labour.

    D Group leadership.

    E Group size.

Questions 29–30

Choose **TWO** letters, **A–E**.

Which **TWO** problems does Sam identify concerning the lecturers?

- **A** Punctuality.
- **B** Organisation.
- **C** Accessibility.
- **D** Helpfulness.
- **E** Teaching materials.

<table>
<tr><td>**SECTION 4**</td><td>**Questions 31–40**</td></tr>
</table>

Questions 31–40

Complete the notes below.

Write **ONE WORD ONLY** for each answer.

The Tawny Owl

Most **31** .... owl species in UK

Strongly nocturnal

<u>Habitat</u>

Mainly lives in **32** .... , but can also be seen in urban areas, e.g. parks.

<u>Adaptations:</u>

- Short wings and **33** .... , for navigation

- Brown and **34** .... feathers, for camouflage

- Large eyes (more effective than those of **35** ....), for good night vision

- Very good spatial **36** .... , for predicting where prey might be found

- Excellent **37** .... , for locating prey from a perch

<u>Diet</u>

Main food is small mammals.

Owls in urban areas eat more **38** ....

<u>Survival</u>

Two thirds of young owls die within a **39** ....

Owls don't disperse over long distances.

Owls seem to dislike flying over large areas of **40** ....

---

*You should spend about 20 minutes on **Questions 1–13**, which are based on Reading Passage 1 below.*

The economic importance of coral reefs

A lot of people around the world are dependent, or partly dependent, on coral reefs for their livelihoods. They often live adjacent to the reef, and their livelihood revolves around the direct extraction, processing and sale of reef resources such as shell fish and seaweeds. In addition, their homes are sheltered by the reef from wave action.

Reef flats and shallow reef lagoons are accessible on foot, without the need for a boat, and so allow women, children and the elderly to engage directly in manual harvesting, or 'reef-gleaning'. This is a significant factor distinguishing reef-based fisheries from near-shore sea fisheries. Near-shore fisheries are typically the domain of adult males, in particular where they involve the use of boats, with women and children restricted mainly to shore-based activities. However, in a coral-reef fishery the physical accessibility of the reef opens up opportunities for direct participation by women, and consequently increases their independence and the importance of their role in the community. It also provides a place for children to play, and to acquire important skills and knowledge for later in life. For example, in the South West Island of Tobi, in the Pacific Ocean, young boys use simple hand lines with a loop and bait at the end to develop the art of fishing on the reef. Similarly, in the Surin Islands of Thailand, young Moken boys spend much of their time playing, swimming and diving in shallow reef lagoons, and in doing so build crucial skills for their future daily subsistence.

Secondary occupations, such as fish processing and marketing activities, are often dominated by women, and offer an important survival strategy for households with access to few other physical assets (such as boats and gear), for elderly women, widows, or the wives of infirm men. On Ulithi Atoll in the western Pacific, women have a distinct role and rights in the distribution of fish catches. This is because the canoes, made from mahogany logs from nearby Yap Island, are obtained through the exchange of cloth made by the women of Ulithi. Small-scale reef fisheries support the involvement of local women traders and their involvement can give them greater control over the household income, and in negotiating for loans or credit. Thus their role is not only important in providing income for their families, it also underpins the economy of the local village.

Poor people with little access to land, labour and financial resources are particularly reliant on exploiting natural resources, and consequently they are vulnerable to seasonal changes in availability of those resources. The diversity of coral reef fisheries, combined with their physical accessibility and the protection they provide against bad weather, make them relatively stable compared with other fisheries, or land-based agricultural production.

In many places, the reef may even act as a resource bank, used as a means of saving food for future times of need. In Manus, Papua New Guinea, giant clams are collected and held in walled enclosures on the reef, until they are needed during periods of rough weather. In Palau, sea cucumbers are seldom eaten during good weather in an effort to conserve their populations for months during which rough weather prohibits good fishing.

Coral reef resources also act as a buffer against seasonal lows in other sectors, particularly agriculture. For example, in coastal communities in northern Mozambique, reef harvests provide key sources of food and cash when agricultural production is low, with the peak in fisheries production coinciding with the period of lowest agricultural stocks. In Papua New Guinea, while agriculture is the primary means of food production, a large proportion of the coastal population engage in sporadic subsistence fishing.

In many coral-reef areas, tourism is one of the main industries bringing employment, and in many cases is promoted to provide alternatives to fisheries-based livelihoods, and to ensure that local reef resources are conserved. In the Caribbean alone, tours based on scuba-diving have attracted 20 million people in one year. The upgrading of roads and communications associated with the expansion of tourism may also bring benefits to local communities. However, plans for development must be considered carefully. The ability of the poorer members of the community to access the benefits of tourism is far from guaranteed, and requires development guided by social, cultural and environmental principles. There is growing recognition that sustainability is a key requirement, as encompassed in small-scale eco-tourism activities, for instance.

Where tourism development has not been carefully planned, and the needs and priorities of the local community have not been properly recognised, conflict has sometimes arisen between tourism and local, small-scale fishers.

Questions 1–7

Do the following statements agree with the information given in Reading Passage 1?

Write

TRUE   if the statement agrees with the information
FALSE   if the statement contradicts the information
NOT GIVEN   if there is no information on this

1   In most places, coral-reef gleaning is normally carried out by men.

2   Involvement in coral-reef-based occupations raises the status of women.

3   Coral reefs provide valuable learning opportunities for young children.

4   The women of Ulithi Atoll have some control over how fish catches are shared out.

5   Boats for use by the inhabitants of Ulithi are constructed on Yap Island.

6   In coral reef fisheries, only male traders can apply for finance.

7   Coral reefs provide a less constant source of income than near-shore seas.

Questions 8–13

Complete the notes below.

*Choose **NO MORE THAN TWO WORDS** from the passage for each answer.*

How coral-reef-based resources protect people during difficult times

Coral reefs can provide

- a resource bank, e.g. for keeping clams and **8** ....

- a seasonal back-up, when **9** .... products are insufficient, e.g. in northern Mozambique.

- a tourist attraction, e.g. **10** .... tours in the Caribbean.

Benefits for local people include:

- The creation of jobs.

- Improvements to roads and **11** ....

Important considerations:

- Development must be based on appropriate principles.

- Need for **12** ....

- Poorly-planned development can create **13** .... with local fishers.

You should spend about 20 minutes on **Questions 14–26**, which are based on Reading Passage 2 on pages 105–106.

Questions 14–26

Questions 14–19

Reading Passage 2 has **SIX** paragraphs, **A–F**.

Choose the correct heading for paragraphs **A–F** from the list of headings below.

Write the correct number, **i–ix**.

List of Headings

i	A suggested modification to a theory about learning.
ii	The problem of superficial understanding.
iii	The relationship between scientific understanding and age.
iv	The rejection of a widely held theory.
v	The need to develop new concepts in daily life.
vi	The claim that a perceived contradiction can assist mental development.
vii	Implications for the training of science teachers.
viii	An experiment to assess the benefits of exchanging views with a partner.
ix	Evidence for the delayed benefits of disagreement between pupils.

---

14 Paragraph **A**   ....

15 Paragraph **B**   ....

16 Paragraph **C**   ....

17 Paragraph **D**   ....

18 Paragraph **E**   ....

19 Paragraph **F**   ....

Acquiring the principles of mathematics and science

A It has been pointed out that learning mathematics and science is not so much learning facts as learning ways of thinking. It has also been emphasised that in order to learn science, people often have to change the way they think in ordinary situations. For example, in order to understand even simple concepts such as heat and temperature, ways of thinking of temperature as a measure of heat must be abandoned and a distinction between 'temperature' and 'heat' must be learned. These changes in ways of thinking are often referred to as conceptual changes. But how do conceptual changes happen? How do young people change their ways of thinking as they develop and as they learn in school?

B Traditional instruction based on telling students how modern scientists think does not seem to be very successful. Students may learn the definitions, the formulae, the terminology, and yet still maintain their previous conceptions. This difficulty has been illustrated many times, for example, when instructed students are interviewed about heat and temperature. It is often identified by teachers as a difficulty in applying the concepts learned in the classroom; students may be able to repeat a formula but fail to use the concept represented by the formula when they explain observed events.

C The psychologist Piaget suggested an interesting hypothesis relating to the process of cognitive change in children. Cognitive change was expected to result from the pupils' own intellectual activity. When confronted with a result that challenges their thinking – that is, when faced with conflict – pupils realise that they need to think again about their own ways of solving problems, regardless of whether the problem is one in mathematics or in science. He hypothesised that conflict brings about disequilibrium, and then triggers equilibration processes that ultimately produce cognitive change. For this reason, according to Piaget and his colleagues, in order for pupils to progress in their thinking they need to be actively engaged in solving problems that will challenge their current mode of reasoning. However, Piaget also pointed out that young children do not always discard their ideas in the face of contradictory evidence. They may actually discard the evidence and keep their theory.

D Piaget's hypothesis about how cognitive change occurs was later translated into an educational approach which is now termed 'discovery learning'. Discovery learning initially took what is now considered the 'lone learner' route. The role of the teacher was to select situations that challenged the pupils' reasoning; and the pupils' peers had no real role in this process. However, it was subsequently proposed that interpersonal conflict, especially with peers, might play an important role in promoting cognitive change. This hypothesis, originally advanced by Perret-Clermont (1980) and Doise and Mugny (1984), has been investigated in many recent studies of science teaching and learning.

E Christine Howe and her colleagues, for example, have compared children's progress in understanding several types of science concepts when they are given the opportunity to observe relevant events. In one study, Howe compared the progress of 8 to 12-year-old children in understanding what influences motion down a slope. In order to ascertain the role of conflict in group work, they created two kinds of groups according to a pre-test: one in which the children had dissimilar views, and a second in which the children had similar views.

They found support for the idea that children in the groups with dissimilar views progressed more after their training sessions than those who had been placed in groups with similar views. However, they found no evidence to support the idea that the children worked out their new conceptions *during* their group discussions, because progress was not actually observed in a post-test immediately after the sessions of group work, but rather in a second test given around four weeks *after* the group work.

F   In another study, Howe set out to investigate whether the progress obtained through pair work could be a function of the exchange of ideas. They investigated the progress made by 12–15-year-old pupils in understanding the path of falling objects, a topic that usually involves conceptual difficulties. In order to create pairs of pupils with varying levels of dissimilarity in their initial conceptions, the pupils' predictions and explanations of the path of falling objects were assessed before they were engaged in pair work. The work sessions involved solving computer-presented problems, again about predicting and explaining the paths of falling objects. A post-test, given to individuals, assessed the progress made by pupils in their conceptions of what influenced the path of falling objects.

Questions 20–21

*Choose **TWO** letters, **A–E**.*

The list below contains some possible statements about learning.

Which **TWO** of these statements are attributed to Piaget by the writer of the passage?

    A Teachers can assist learning by explaining difficult concepts.

    B Mental challenge is a stimulus to learning.

    C Repetition and consistency of input aid cognitive development.

    D Children sometimes reject evidence that conflicts with their preconceptions.

    E Children can help each other make cognitive progress.

Questions 22–23

*Choose **TWO** letters, **A–E**.*

Which **TWO** of these statements describe Howe's experiment with 8–12-year-olds?

    A The children were assessed on their ability to understand a scientific problem.

    B All the children were working in mixed-ability groups.

    C The children who were the most talkative made the least progress.

    D The teacher helped the children to understand a scientific problem.

    E The children were given a total of three tests, at different times.

Questions 24–26

Complete the summary below.

*Choose **NO MORE THAN TWO WORDS** from the passage for each answer.*

How children learn

Piaget proposed that learning takes place when children encounter ideas that do not correspond to their current beliefs. The application of this theory gave rise to a teaching method known as **24** .... At first this approach only focused on the relationship between individual pupils and their **25** .... Later, researchers such as Perret-Clermont became interested in the role that interaction with **26** .... might also play in a pupil's development.

Learning lessons from the past

Many past societies collapsed or vanished, leaving behind monumental ruins such as those that the poet Shelley imagined in his sonnet, *Ozymandias*. By collapse, I mean a drastic decrease in human population size and/or political/economic/social complexity, over a considerable area, for an extended time. By those standards, most people would consider the following past societies to have been famous victims of full-fledged collapses rather than of just minor declines: the Anasazi and Cahokia within the boundaries of the modern US, the Maya cities in Central America, Moche and Tiwanaku societies in South America, Norse Greenland, Mycenean Greece and Minoan Crete in Europe, Great Zimbabwe in Africa, Angkor Wat and the Harappan Indus Valley cities in Asia, and Easter Island in the Pacific Ocean.

The monumental ruins left behind by those past societies hold a fascination for all of us. We marvel at them when as children we first learn of them through pictures. When we grow up, many of us plan vacations in order to experience them at first hand. We feel drawn to their often spectacular and haunting beauty, and also to the mysteries that they pose. The scales of the ruins testify to the former wealth and power of their builders. Yet these builders vanished, abandoning the great structures that they had created at such effort. How could a society that was once so mighty end up collapsing?

It has long been suspected that many of those mysterious abandonments were at least partly triggered by ecological problems: people inadvertently destroying the environmental resources on which their societies depended. This suspicion of unintended ecological suicide (ecocide) has been confirmed by discoveries made in recent decades by archaeologists, climatologists, historians, paleontologists, and palynologists (pollen scientists). The processes through which past societies have undermined themselves by damaging their environments fall into eight categories, whose relative importance differs from case to case: deforestation and habitat destruction, soil problems, water management problems, overhunting, overfishing, effects of introduced species on native species, human population growth, and increased impact of people.

Those past collapses tended to follow somewhat similar courses constituting variations on a theme. Writers find it tempting to draw analogies between the course of human societies and the course of individual human lives – to talk of a society's birth, growth, peak, old age and eventual death. But that metaphor proves erroneous for many past societies: they declined rapidly after reaching peak numbers and power, and those rapid declines must have come as a surprise and shock to their citizens. Obviously, too, this trajectory is not one that all past societies followed unvaryingly to completion: different societies collapsed to different degrees and in somewhat different ways, while many societies did not collapse at all.

Today many people feel that environmental problems overshadow all the other threats to global civilisation. These environmental problems include the same eight that undermined past societies, plus four new ones: human-caused climate change, build up of toxic chemicals in the environment, energy shortages, and full human utilisation of the Earth's photosynthetic capacity. But the seriousness of these current environmental problems is vigorously debated. Are the risks greatly exaggerated, or conversely are they underestimated? Will modern technology solve our problems, or is it creating new problems faster than it solves old ones? When we deplete one resource (e.g. wood, oil, or ocean fish), can we count on being able to substitute some new resource (e.g. plastics, wind and solar energy, or farmed fish)? Isn't the rate of human population growth declining, such that we're already on course for the world's population to level off at some manageable number of people?

Questions like this illustrate why those famous collapses of past civilisations have taken on more meaning than just that of a romantic mystery. Perhaps there are some practical lessons that we could learn from all those past collapses. But there are also differences between the modern world and its problems, and those past societies and their problems. We shouldn't be so naïve as to think that study of the past will yield simple solutions, directly transferable to our societies today. We differ from past societies in some respects that put us at lower risk than them; some of those respects often mentioned include our powerful technology (i.e. its beneficial effects), globalisation, modern medicine, and greater knowledge of past societies and of distant modern societies. We also differ from past societies in some respects that put us at greater risk than them: again, our potent technology (i.e., its unintended destructive effects), globalisation (such that now a problem in one part of the world affects all the rest), the dependence of millions of us on modern medicine for our survival, and our much larger human population. Perhaps we can still learn from the past, but only if we think carefully about its lessons.

Questions 27–40

Questions 27–29

*Choose the correct letter, **A**, **B**, **C** or **D**.*

27 When the writer describes the impact of monumental ruins today, he emphasises

    A the income they generate from tourism.

    B the area of land they occupy.

    C their archaeological value.

    D their romantic appeal.

28 Recent findings concerning vanished civilisations have

    A overturned long-held beliefs.

    B caused controversy amongst scientists.

    C come from a variety of disciplines.

    D identified one main cause of environmental damage.

29 What does the writer say about ways in which former societies collapsed?

    A The pace of decline was usually similar.

    B The likelihood of collapse would have been foreseeable.

    C Deterioration invariably led to total collapse.

    D Individual citizens could sometimes influence the course of events.

Questions 30–34

Do the following statements agree with the views of the writer in Reading Passage 3?

Write

YES   *if the statement agrees with the claims of the writer*
NO   *if the statement contradicts the claims of the writer*
NOT GIVEN   *if it is impossible to say what the writer thinks about this*

30 It is widely believed that environmental problems represent the main danger faced by the modern world.

31 The accumulation of poisonous substances is a relatively modern problem.

32 There is general agreement that the threats posed by environmental problems are very serious.

33 Some past societies resembled present-day societies more closely than others.

34 We should be careful when drawing comparisons between past and present.

Questions 35–39

Complete each sentence with the correct ending, **A–F**, below.

Write the correct letter, **A–F**.

35 Evidence of the greatness of some former civilisations

36 The parallel between an individual's life and the life of a society

37 The number of environmental problems that societies face

38 The power of technology

39 A consideration of historical events and trends

    A is not necessarily valid.

    B provides grounds for an optimistic outlook.

    C exists in the form of physical structures.

    D is potentially both positive and negative.

    E will not provide direct solutions for present problems.

    F is greater now than in the past.

Question 40

Choose the correct letter, **A**, **B**, **C** or **D**.

40 What is the main argument of Reading Passage **3**?

    A There are differences as well as similarities between past and present societies.

    B More should be done to preserve the physical remains of earlier civilisations.

    C Some historical accounts of great civilisations are inaccurate.

    D Modern societies are dependent on each other for their continuing survival.

Writing module (1 hour)

You should spend about 20 minutes on this task.

> **The graph and bar chart below show the average monthly rainfall and temperature for one region of East Africa.**
>
> **Summarise the information by selecting and reporting the main features, and making comparisons where relevant.**

Write at least 150 words.

Average monthly rainfall and temperatures

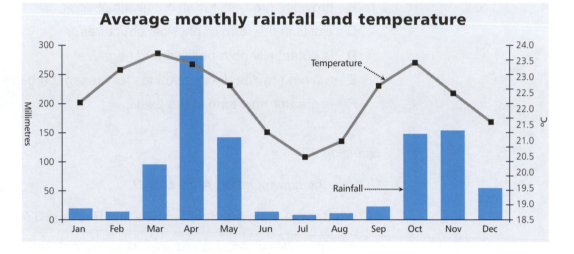

WRITING TASK 2   You should spend about 40 minutes on this task.

Write about the following topic:

> **Meat production requires relatively more land than crop production. Some people think that as land is becoming scarce, the world's meat consumption should be reduced.**
>
> **What measures could be taken to reduce the world's meat consumption? What kinds of problem might such measures cause?**

Give reasons for your answer, and include any relevant examples from your own knowledge or experience.

Write at least 250 words.

Speaking module (11–14 minutes)

PART 1

Answer these questions.

Let's talk about what you do.

Do you work, or are you a student?
EITHER
How much time do you spend studying each day? Why/Why not?
Do you sometimes work in a group with other students? Why/Why not?
OR
What is the length of your normal working day?
Do you sometimes work in a team? Why/Why not?

Now let's talk about computer games.

Do you prefer playing computer games alone or with a friend? Why/Why not?
At what age did you first play computer games? Why/Why not?
Do you ever buy computer games for other people? Why/Why not?
In general, are computer games more popular with men or with women? Why?

PART 2

You have one minute to make notes on the following topic. Then you have up to two minutes to talk about it.

Describe the room in your house/apartment which you like best.

You should say:

      where the room is

      what it is used for

      what it looks like

and explain why you like this room best.

Do other people like this room?
Do you spend much time there?

PART 3

Consider these questions, and then answer them.

Now let's talk about rooms in general.

Which room do families usually spend most time in? Why?
What types of thing do people usually put on the walls of their rooms?
Is it more important for a room to look nice, or to be comfortable? Why?

Let's go on to talk about interior design.

How can different room colours affect the way people feel?
What is modern furniture like compared to older styles of furniture?
Do you think women are more interested than men in the way rooms are decorated? Why/Why not?

Let's discuss indoor and outdoor living spaces next.

How might the climate of an area affect the importance of indoor and outdoor living spaces? Why?
What do you think living spaces will be like in the future? Why?

TEST 6

Listening module (approx 30 minutes + 10 minutes transfer time)

Questions 1–10

Complete the table below.

*Write **ONE WORD AND/OR A NUMBER** for each answer.*

HOLIDAY RENTALS	Dates: Example	.....10th–22nd July.....		
Name of Property	Location	Features	Disadvantage(s)	Booking details
1	• rural • surrounded by **2**	• apartment • two bedrooms • open plan	distance from **3**	www. **4** .... com

Kingfisher	• rural
	• next to the
	  5 ....
	• nice views
		• house
		• three bedrooms
		• **6** ....
		  room
		• living room
		• kitchen
			expensive?	Phone the owner (01752 669218)

Sunnybanks	• in a village
	• next to the
	  7 ....
		• house
		• has private
		  8 ....
			no
			9 ....
				Contact the
				10 ....

Questions 11–20

Questions 11–14

*Choose the correct letter, **A**, **B** or **C**.*

11 According to the speaker, why is it a good time for D-I-Y painting?

    A There are better products available now.

    B Materials cost less than they used to.

    C People have more free time than before.

12 What happened in 2009 in the UK?

    A A record volume of paint was sold.

    B A large amount of paint was wasted.

    C There was a major project to repaint public buildings.

13 What does the speaker say about paint quantity?

    A It's not necessary to have exact room measurements.

    B It's better to overestimate than to underestimate.

    C An automatic calculator can be downloaded from the Internet.

14 What does Community RePaint do?

    A It paints people's houses without payment.

    B It collects unwanted paint and gives it away.

    C It sells unused paint and donates the money to charity.

Questions 15–16

Choose *TWO* letters, *A–E*.

What **TWO** pieces of advice does the speaker give about paint?

    A Don't buy expensive paint.

    B Test the colour before buying a lot.

    C Choose a light colour.

    D Use water-based paint.

    E Buy enough paint for more than one application.

Questions 17–18

Choose **TWO** *letters,* **A–E**.

What **TWO** pieces of advice does the speaker give about preparation?

    A Replace any loose plaster.

    B Don't spend too long preparing surfaces.

    C Use decorators' soap to remove grease from walls.

    D Wash dirty walls with warm water.

    E Paint over cracks and small holes.

Questions 19–20

Choose **TWO** *letters,* **A–E**.

What **TWO** pieces of advice does the speaker give about painting?

    A Put a heater in the room.

    B Wash brushes in cold water.

    C Use a roller with a short pile.

    D Apply paint directly from the tin.

    E Open doors and windows.

Questions 21–30

Questions 21–26

*Choose the correct letter, **A**, **B** or **C**.*

21 Why is Matthew considering a student work placement?

    A He was informed about an interesting vacancy.

    B He needs some extra income.

    C He wants to try out a career option.

22 Which part of the application process did Linda find most interesting?

    A The psychometric test.

    B The group activity.

    C The individual task.

23 During her work placement, Linda helped find ways to

    A speed up car assembly.

    B process waste materials.

    C calculate the cost of design faults.

24 Why did Linda find her work placement tiring?

    A She wasn't used to full-time work.

    B The working hours were very long.

    C She felt she had to prove her worth.

25 What did Linda's employers give her formal feedback on?

    A engineering ability

    B organisational skills

    C team working

26 What was the main benefit of Linda's work placement?

    A Improved academic skills.

    B An offer of work.

    C The opportunity to use new software.

Questions 27–30

What does Linda think about the books on Matthew's reading list?

*Choose **FOUR** answers from the box and write the correct letter, **A–F**, next to questions 27–30.*

Opinions

A   helpful illustrations

B   easy to understand

C   up-to-date

D   comprehensive

E   specialised

F   useful case studies

Books

27   *The Science of Materials*   ....

28   *Materials Engineering*   ....

29   *Engineering Basics*   ....

30   *Evolution of Materials*   ....

Questions 31–40

Complete the notes below.

Write **NO MORE THAN TWO WORDS** for each answer.

Researching the origin of medieval manuscripts

Background

- Medieval manuscripts – handwritten books produced between the fifth and fifteenth centuries

- Origin of many manuscripts unknown until 2009; scientists started using DNA testing

Animal hides – two types

Parchment

Sheep skin: white in colour and **31** ....

Greasy – writing can't be erased so often used for **32** ....

Vellum

Calf skin: most popular for prestigious work because you can get **33** .... lettering.

Preparation of hides

- Treated in barrels of lime – where this was not available, skins were **34**. .... (removed hair → more flexible)

- Stretched tight on a frame

- Scraped to create same **35** ....

- Vellum was **36** .... – for correct colour

Genetic testing – finding origins

Previously – analysed handwriting and **37** .... used by the writer

Now – using genetic data from 'known manuscripts' to create a **38** ' .... '

Uses of new data

Gives information on individual books

Shows the **39** .... of the book industry

Helps define **40** .... in medieval period

Trends in the Indian fashion and textile industries

During the 1950s, the Indian fashion scene was exciting, stylish and very graceful. There were no celebrity designers or models, nor were there any labels that were widely recognised. The value of a garment was judged by its style and fabric rather than by who made it. It was regarded as perfectly acceptable, even for high-society women, to approach an unknown tailor who could make a garment for a few rupees, providing the perfect fit, finish and style. They were proud of getting a bargain, and of giving their own name to the end result.

The 1960s was an era full of mischievousness and celebration in the arts, music and cinema. The period was characterised by freedom from restrictions and, in the fashion world, an acceptance of innovative types of material such as plastic and coated polyester. Tight-fitting *kurtas** and *churidars*** and high coiffures were a trend among women.

The following decade witnessed an increase in the export of traditional materials, and the arrival in India of international fashion. Synthetics became trendy, and the disco culture affected the fashion scene.

It was in the early 80s when the first fashion store 'Ravissant' opened in Mumbai. At that time garments were retailed for a four-figure price tag. American designers like Calvin Klein became popular. In India too, contours became more masculine, and even the *salwar kameez**** was designed with shoulder pads.

With the evolution of designer stores came the culture of designer fashion, along with its hefty price tags. Whatever a garment was like, consumers were convinced that a higher price tag signified elegant designer fashion, so garments were sold at unbelievable prices. Meanwhile, designers decided to get themselves noticed by making showy outfits and associating with the right celebrities. Soon, fashion shows became competitive, each designer attempting to out-do the other in theme, guest list and media coverage.

In the last decade of the millennium, the market shrank and ethnic wear made a comeback. During the recession, there was a push to sell at any cost. With fierce competition the inevitable occurred: the once hefty price tags began their downward journey, and the fashion-show industry followed suit. However, the liveliness of the Indian fashion scene had not ended – it had merely reached a stable level.

At the beginning of the 21st century, with new designers and models, and more sensible designs, the fashion industry accelerated once again. As far as the global fashion industry is concerned, Indian ethnic designs and materials are currently in demand from fashion houses and garment manufacturers. India is the third largest producer of cotton, the second largest producer of silk, and the fifth largest producer of man-made fibres in the world.

The Indian garment and fabric industries have many fundamental advantages, in terms of a cheaper, skilled work force, cost-effective production, raw materials, flexibility, and a wide range of designs with sequins, beadwork, and embroidery. In addition, that India provides garments to international fashion houses at competitive prices, with a shorter lead time, and an effective monopoly on certain designs, is accepted the whole world over. India has always been regarded as the default source in the embroidered garments segment, but changes in the rate of exchange between the rupee and the dollar has further depressed prices, thereby attracting more buyers. So the international fashion houses walk away with customised goods, and craftwork is sold at very low rates.

As far as the fabric market is concerned, the range available in India can attract as well as confuse the buyer. Much of the production takes place in the small town of Chapa in the eastern state of Bihar, a name one might never have heard of. Here fabric-making is a family industry; the range and quality of raw silks churned out here belie the crude production methods and equipment. Surat in Gujarat, is the supplier of an amazing set of jacquards, moss crepes and georgette sheers – all fabrics in high demand. Another Indian fabric design that has been adopted by the fashion industry is the 'Madras check', originally utilised for the universal *lungi*, a simple lower-body wrap worn in southern India. This design has now found its way on to bandannas, blouses, home furnishings and almost anything one can think of.

Ethnic Indian designs with *batik* and hand-embroidered motifs have also become popular across the world. Decorative bead work is another product in demand in the international market. Beads are used to prepare accessory items like belts and bags, and beadwork is now available for haute couture evening wear too.

---

*	knee-length tunics
**	trousers
***	trouser suit

Questions 1–7

Complete the notes below.

Choose **ONE WORD ONLY** from the passage for each answer.

Indian fashion: 1950–2000

1950s

- No well-known designers, models or **1** ....

- Elegant clothing cost little

- Women were pleased to get clothes for a **2** .... price

1960s

- New materials, e.g. **3** .... and polyester

- Fitted clothing and tall hairstyles

1970s

- Overseas sales of **4** .... fabrics rose

- Influence of international fashion

1980s

- Opening of fashion store in Mumbai

- Popularity of American designers

- Clothing had a **5** .... shape

- Designers tried to attract attention by presenting **6** .... clothes and mixing with stars

1990s

- Fall in demand for expensive fashion wear

- Return to **7**.................. clothing

Questions 8–13

Do the following statements agree with the information given in Reading Passage 1?

Write

TRUE   *if the statement agrees with the information*
FALSE   *if the statement contradicts the information*
NOT GIVEN *if there is no information on this*

8   At the start of the 21st century, key elements in the Indian fashion industry changed.

9   India now exports more than half of the cotton it produces.

10 Conditions in India are generally well suited to the manufacture of clothing.

11 Indian clothing exports have suffered from changes in the value of its currency.

12 Modern machinery accounts for the high quality of Chapa's silk.

13 Some types of Indian craftwork which are internationally popular had humble origins.

Sustainable growth at Didcot: the outline of a report by South Oxfordshire District Council

A

The UK Government's South East Plan proposes additional housing growth in the town of Didcot, which has been a designated growth area since 1979. We in South Oxfordshire District Council consider that, although Didcot does have potential for further growth, such development should be sustainable, well-planned, and supported by adequate infrastructure and community services.

B

Recent experience in Didcot has demonstrated that large greenfield* developments cannot resource all the necessary infrastructure and low-cost housing requirements. The ensuing compromises create a legacy of local transport, infrastructure and community services deficits, with no obvious means of correction. We wish to ensure that there is greater recognition of the cost attached to housing growth, and that a means is found to resource the establishment of sustainable communities in growth areas.

C

Until the 1950s, the development of job opportunities in the railway industry, and in a large, military ordnance depot, was the spur to Didcot's expansion. Development at that time was geared to providing homes for the railway and depot workers, with limited investment in shopping and other services for the local population. Didcot failed to develop Broadway as a compact town centre, and achieved only a strip of shops along one side of the main street hemmed in by low density housing and service trade uses.

D

From the 1970s, strategic planning policies directed significant new housing development to Didcot. Planners recognised Didcot's potential, with rapid growth in local job opportunities and good rail connections for those choosing to work farther afield. However, the town is bisected by the east–west railway, and people living in Ladygrove, the urban extension to the north which has been built since the 1980s, felt, and still feel, cut off from the town and its community.

E

Population growth in the new housing areas failed to spark adequate private-sector investment in town centre uses, and the limited investment which did take place – Didcot Market Place development in 1982, for instance – did not succeed in delivering the number and range of town centre uses needed by the growing population. In 1990, public-sector finance was used to buy the land required for the Orchard Centre development, comprising a superstore, parking and a new street of stores running parallel to Broadway. The development took 13 years to complete.

F

The idea that, by obliging developers of new housing to contribute to the cost of infrastructure and service requirements, all the necessary finance could be raised, has proved unachievable. Substantial public finance was still needed to deliver major projects such as the new link road to the A34 on the outskirts of the town at Milton, the improved railway crossing at Marsh Bridge and new schools. Such projects were delayed due to difficulties in securing public finance. The same problem also held back expansion of health and social services in the town.

G

In recent years, government policy, in particular the requirement for developers that forty percent of the units in a new housing development should be low cost homes, has had a major impact on the economics of such development, as it has limited the developers' contribution to the costs of infrastructure. The planning authorities are facing difficult choices in prioritising the items of infrastructure which must be funded by development, and this, in turn, means that from now on public finance will need to provide a greater proportion of infrastructure project costs.

H

The Government's Sustainable Communities Plan seeks a holistic approach to new urban development in which housing, employment, services and infrastructure of all kinds are carefully planned and delivered in a way which avoids the infrastructure deficits that have occurred in places like Didcot in the past. This report, therefore, is structured around the individual components of a sustainable community, and shows the baseline position for each component.

I

Didcot has been identified as one of the towns with which the Government is working to evaluate whether additional growth will strengthen the economic potential of the town, deliver the necessary infrastructure and improve environmental standards. A programme of work, including discussions with the local community about their aspirations for the town as well as other stakeholders, will be undertaken over the coming months, and will lead to the development of a strategic master plan. The challenge will be in optimising scarce resources to achieve maximum benefits for the town.

---

*   land that has never previously been built on

Questions 14–26

Questions 14–19

*Reading Passage 2 has nine paragraphs, **A–I**.*

Which paragraph contains the following information?

*Write the correct letter, **A–I**.*

14 reference to the way the council's report is organised

15 the reason why inhabitants in one part of Didcot are isolated

16 a statement concerning future sources of investment

17 the identification of two major employers at Didcot

18 reference to groups who will be consulted about a new development plan

19 an account of how additional town centre facilities were previously funded

Questions 20–23

Look at the following places and the list of statements below.

*Match each place with the correct statement, **A–F**.*

*Write the correct letter, **A–F**.*

20 Broadway

21 Market Place

22 Orchard Centre

23 Marsh Bridge

List of statements

A It provided extra facilities for shopping and cars.

B Its location took a long time to agree.

C Its layout was unsuitable.

D Its construction was held up due to funding problems.

E It was privately funded.

F It failed to get Council approval at first.

Questions 24–26

Complete the sentences below.

Choose **NO MORE THAN THREE WORDS** *from the passage for each answer.*

24 A certain proportion of houses in any new development now have to be of the ……………… type.

25 The government is keen to ensure that adequate ……………… will be provided for future housing developments.

26 The views of Didcot's inhabitants and others will form the basis of a ……………… for the town.

Language diversity

One of the most influential ideas in the study of languages is that of universal grammar (UG). Put forward by Noam Chomsky in the 1960s, it is widely interpreted as meaning that all languages are basically the same, and that the human brain is born language-ready, with an in-built programme that is able to interpret the common rules underlying any mother tongue. For five decades this idea prevailed, and influenced work in linguistics, psychology and cognitive science. To understand language, it implied, you must sweep aside the huge diversity of languages, and find their common human core.

Since the theory of UG was proposed, linguists have identified many universal language rules. However, there are almost always exceptions. It was once believed, for example, that if a language had syllables* that begin with a vowel and end with a consonant (VC), it would also have syllables that begin with a consonant and end with a vowel (CV). This universal lasted until 1999, when linguists showed that Arrernte, spoken by Indigenous Australians from the area around Alice Springs in the Northern Territory, has VC syllables but no CV syllables.

Other non-universal universals describe the basic rules of putting words together. Take the rule that every language contains four basic word classes: nouns, verbs, adjectives and adverbs. Work in the past two decades has shown that several languages lack an open adverb class, which means that new adverbs cannot be readily formed, unlike in English where you can turn any adjective into an adverb, for example 'soft' into 'softly'. Others, such as Lao, spoken in Laos, have no adjectives at all. More controversially, some linguists argue that a few languages, such as Straits Salish, spoken by indigenous people from north-western regions of North America, do not even have distinct nouns or verbs. Instead, they have a single class of words to include events, objects and qualities.

Even apparently indisputable universals have been found lacking. This includes recursion, or the ability to infinitely place one grammatical unit inside a similar unit, such as 'Jack thinks that Mary thinks that … the bus will be on time'. It is widely considered to be the most essential characteristic of human language, one that sets it apart from the communications of all other animals. Yet Dan Everett at Illinois State University recently published controversial work showing that Amazonian Piraha does not have this quality.

But what if the very diversity of languages is the key to understanding human communication? Linguists Nicholas Evans of the Australian National University in Canberra, and Stephen Levinson of the Max Planck Institute for Psycholinguistics in Nijmegen, the Netherlands, believe that languages do not share a common set of rules. Instead, they say, their sheer variety is a defining feature of human communication – something not seen in other animals. While there is no doubt that human thinking influences the form that language takes, if Evans and Levinson are correct, language in turn shapes our brains. This suggests that humans are more diverse than we thought, with our brains having differences depending on the language environment in which we grew up. And that leads to a disturbing conclusion: every time a language becomes extinct, humanity loses an important piece of diversity.

If languages do not obey a single set of shared rules, then how are they created? 'Instead of universals, you get standard engineering solutions that languages adopt again and again, and then you get outliers,' says Evans. He and Levinson argue that this is because any given language is a complex system shaped by many factors, including culture, genetics and history. There are no absolutely universal traits of language, they say, only tendencies. And it is a mix of strong and weak tendencies that characterises the 'bio-cultural' mix that we call language.

According to the two linguists, the strong tendencies explain why many languages display common patterns. A variety of factors tend to push language in a similar direction, such as the structure of the brain, the biology of speech, and the efficiencies of communication. Widely shared linguistic elements may also be ones that build on a particularly human kind of reasoning. For example, the fact that before we learn to speak we perceive the world as a place full of things causing actions (agents) and things having actions done to them (patients) explains why most languages deploy these grammatical categories.

Weak tendencies, in contrast, are explained by the idiosyncrasies of different languages. Evans and Levinson argue that many aspects of the particular natural history of a population may affect its language. For instance, Andy Butcher at Flinders University in Adelaide, South Australia, has observed that indigenous Australian children have by far the highest incidence of chronic middle-ear infection of any population on the planet, and that most indigenous Australian languages lack many sounds that are common in other languages, but which are hard to hear with a middle-ear infection. Whether this condition has shaped the sound systems of these languages is unknown, says Evans, but it is important to consider the idea.

Levinson and Evans are not the first to question the theory of universal grammar, but no one has summarised these ideas quite as persuasively, and given them as much reach. As a result, their arguments have generated widespread enthusiasm, particularly among those linguists who are tired of trying to squeeze their findings into the straitjacket of 'absolute universals'. To some, it is the final nail in UG's coffin. Michael Tomasello, co-director of the Max Planck Institute for Evolutionary Anthropology in Leipzig, Germany, has been a long-standing critic of the idea that all languages conform to a set of rules. 'Universal grammar is dead,' he says.

---

* a unit of sound

Questions 27–40

Questions 27–32

Do the following statements agree with the views of the writer in Reading Passage 3?

Write

YES *if the statement agrees with the claims of the writer*
NO *if the statement contradicts the claims of the writer*
NOT GIVEN *if it is impossible to say what the writer thinks about this*

27 In the final decades of the twentieth century, a single theory of language learning was dominant.

28 The majority of UG rules proposed by linguists do apply to all human languages.

29 There is disagreement amongst linguists about an aspect of Straits Salish grammar.

30 The search for new universal language rules has largely ended.

31 If Evans and Levinson are right, people develop in the same way no matter what language they speak.

32 The loss of any single language might have implications for the human race.

Questions 33–37

*Choose the correct letter, **A**, **B**, **C** or **D**.*

33 Which of the following views about language are held by Evans and Levinson?

   A Each of the world's languages develops independently.

   B The differences between languages outweigh the similarities.

   C Only a few language features are universal.

   D Each language is influenced by the characteristics of other languages.

34 According to Evans and Levinson, apparent similarities between languages could be due to

   A close social contact.

   B faulty analysis.

   C shared modes of perception.

   D narrow descriptive systems.

35 In the eighth paragraph, what does the reference to a middle-ear infection serve as?

   A A justification for something.

   B A contrast with something.

   C The possible cause of something.

   D The likely result of something.

36 What does the writer suggest about Evans' and Levinson's theory of language development?

   A It had not been previously considered.

   B It is presented in a convincing way.

   C It has been largely rejected by other linguists.

   D It is not supported by the evidence.

37 Which of the following best describes the writer's purpose?

   A To describe progress in the field of cognitive science.

   B To defend a long-held view of language learning.

   C To identify the similarities between particular languages.

   D To outline opposing views concerning the nature of language.

Questions 38–40

*Complete each sentence with the correct ending, **A–E**, below.*

*Write the correct letter, **A–E**.*

38 The Arrernte language breaks a 'rule' concerning

39 The Lao language has been identified as lacking

40 It has now been suggested that Amazonia Piraha does not have

   A words of a certain grammatical type.

   B a sequence of sounds predicted by UG.

   C words which can have more than one meaning.

   D the language feature regarded as the most basic.

   E sentences beyond a specified length.

Writing module (1 hour)

WRITING TASK 1 *You should spend about 20 minutes on this task.*

> ***Plan A below shows a health centre in 2005. Plan B shows the same place in the present day.***
>
> ***Summarise the information by selecting and reporting the main features, and make comparisons where relevant.***

Write at least 150 words.

CR - Consulting room

WRITING TASK 2 *You should spend about 40 minutes on this task.*

Write about the following topic:

> **Some say that it would be better if the majority of employees worked from home instead of travelling to a workplace every day.**
>
> **Do you think the advantages of working from home outweigh the disadvantages?**

Give reasons for your answer and include any relevant examples from your own knowledge and experience.

Write at least 250 words.

Speaking module (11–14 minutes)

PART 1 Answer these questions.

Let's talk about where you live now.

Do you live near here?
Do you live in a house or an apartment?
How long have you lived there?
Do you like where you are living now? Why/Why not?

Now let's talk about holidays.

How often do you get holiday from work/college?
Do you usually stay at home when you have a holiday, or do you go somewhere? Why/Why not?
What did you do the last time you had a holiday?
Do you wish you had more holidays? Why/Why not?

PART 2 You have one minute to make notes on the following topic. Then you have up to two minutes to talk about it.

Describe a sports match which you saw and which you found enjoyable.

You should say:

> what the sport was
> who was playing in this game
> where you watched it

and explain why you enjoyed watching the match so much.

Do you often watch sport?
Do you do a lot of sport?

PART 3 Consider these questions, and then answer them.

Let's talk about young people doing sports.

What sports do most young people in your country enjoy doing?
What are the main benefits for young people of learning to play different sports?
Can you suggest some ways to encourage young people to play more sport?

Now let's talk about sports on TV.

What kinds of sport do people in your country most often watch on TV? Why?
What do you think are the disadvantages of having a lot of coverage of sports on TV?
How do you think the broadcasting of sports on TV will change in the next 20 years?

Now let's consider international sports competitions.

Why do you think international sports competitions (like the Football World Cup) are so popular?
What are the advantages and disadvantages to a country when it hosts a major international sports competition?
What should governments invest more in: helping their top sports people to win international competitions, or in promoting sport for everyone? Why?

TEST 7

Listening module (approx 30 minutes + 10 minutes transfer time)

SECTION 1

Questions 1–10

Questions 1–10

Complete the notes below.

Write **NO MORE THAN TWO WORDS OR A NUMBER** for each answer.

Notes for holiday

Travel information

Example

Will email the ....flight number......

– *must find out which* **1** .... *arriving at*

– *best taxi company* **2** ....

– *Note: Simon lives in the* **3** .... *of the city*

– *Simon's cell phone number:* **4** ....

What to pack

(to wear)

– *casual clothes*

– *one smart dress – to wear at a* **5** ....

– *a good* **6** ....

– *tough* **7** ....

(to read)

– *try to find book named* **8** ' .... ' *by Rex Campbell.*

(for presents)

– *for Janice:* **9** ....

– *for Alec:* **10** .... *(with racing pictures)*

Questions 11–20

Questions 11–16

Choose the correct answer, **A**, **B** or **C**.

Camber's Theme Park

11 According to the speaker, in what way is Camber's different from other theme parks?

    A It's suitable for different age groups.

    B It offers lots to do in wet weather.

    C It has a focus on education.

12 The Park first opened in

    A 1980.

    B 1997.

    C 2004.

13 What's included in the entrance fee?

    A most rides and parking

    B all rides and some exhibits

    C parking and all rides

14 Becoming a member of the Adventurers Club means

    A you can avoiding queuing so much.

    B you can enter the Park free for a year.

    C you can visit certain zones closed to other people.

15 The Future Farm zone encourages visitors to

    A buy animals as pets.

    B learn about the care of animals.

    C get close to the animals.

16 When is hot food available in the park?

    A 10.00 a.m. – 5.30 p.m.

    B 11.00 a.m. – 5.00 p.m.

    C 10.30 a.m. – 5.00 p.m.

Questions 17–20

What special conditions apply to the following rides?

*Choose **FOUR** answers from the box and write the correct letter, **A–F**, next to the questions 17–20.*

Special conditions for visitors
A Must be over a certain age
B Must use special safety equipment
C Must avoid it if they have health problems
D Must wear a particular type of clothing
E Must be over a certain height
F Must be accompanied by an adult if under 16

Rides

17 River Adventure ....

18 Jungle Jim Rollercoaster ....

19 Swoop Slide ....

20 Zip Go-carts ....

Questions 21–30

Questions 21–22

*Choose **TWO** letters, **A–E**.*

What **TWO** things do Brad and Helen agree to say about listening in groups?

    A Listening skills are often overlooked in business training.

    B Learning to listen well is a skill that's easy for most people to learn.

    C It's sometimes acceptable to argue against speakers.

    D Body language is very important when listening.

    E Listeners should avoid interrupting speakers.

Questions 23–24

*Choose **TWO** letters, **A–E**.*

What **TWO** things does the article say about goal-setting?

    A Meetings should start with a clear statement of goals.

    B It's important for each individual's goals to be explained.

    C Everybody in the group should have the same goals.

    D Goals should be a mix of the realistic and the ideal.

    E Goals must always to be achievable within a set time.

Questions 25–26

*Choose **TWO** letters, **A–E**.*

What **TWO** things do Brad and Helen agree are weak points in the article's section on conflict resolution?

    A It doesn't explore the topic in enough detail.

    B It only discusses conservative views.

    C It says nothing about the potential value of conflict.

    D It talks too much about 'winners and losers'.

    E It doesn't provide definitions of key terms.

Questions 27–30

What actions do Brad and Helen agree to do regarding the following preparation tasks?

*Choose **FOUR** answers from the box and write the correct letter, **A–F**, next to the number.*

Action

A Contact the tutor for clarification.

B Check the assignment specifications.

C Leave it until the last task.

D Ask a course-mate to help.

E Find information on the Internet.

F Look through course handbooks.

Preparation tasks

27 Preparing the powerpoint ....

28 Using direct quotations ....

29 Creating a handout ....

30 Drawing up a bibliography ....

Questions 31–40

Complete the notes below.

Write ONE WORD ONLY for each answer.

Engineering for sustainable development

The Greenhouse Project (Himalayan mountain region)

Problem

- Short growing season because of high altitude and low **31** ....

- Fresh vegetables imported by lorry or by **32** .... , so are expensive

- Need to use sunlight to prevent local plants from **33** ....

- Previous programmes to provide greenhouses were **34** ....

New greenhouse

Meets criteria for sustainability

- Simple and **35** .... to build

- Made mainly from local materials (mud or stone for the walls, wood and **36** .... for the roof)

- Building and maintenance done by local craftsmen

- Runs solely on **37** .... energy

- Only families who have a suitable **38** .... can own one

Design

- Long side faces south

- Strong polythene cover

- Inner **39** .... are painted black or white

Social benefits

- Owners' status is improved

- Rural **40** .... have greater opportunities

- More children are educated

---

*You should spend about 20 minutes on **Questions 1–13**, which are based on Reading Passage 1 below.*

The construction of roads and bridges

Roads

Although there were highway links in Mesopotamia from as early as 3500 BC, the Romans were probably the first road-builders with fixed engineering standards. At the peak of the Roman Empire in the first century AD, Rome had road connections totalling about 85,000 kilometres.

Roman roads were constructed with a deep stone surface for stability and load-bearing. They had straight alignments and therefore were often hilly. The Roman roads remained the main arteries of European transport for many centuries, and even today many roads follow the Roman routes. New roads were generally of inferior quality, and the achievements of Roman builders were largely unsurpassed until the resurgence of road-building in the eighteenth century.

With horse-drawn coaches in mind, eighteenth-century engineers preferred to curve their roads to avoid hills. The road surface was regarded as merely a face to absorb wear, the load-bearing strength being obtained from a properly prepared and well-drained foundation. Immediately above this, the Scottish engineer John McAdam (1756–1836) typically laid crushed stone, to which stone dust mixed with water was added, and which was compacted to a thickness of just five centimetres, and then rolled. McAdam's surface layer – hot tar onto which a layer of stone chips was laid – became known as 'tarmacadam', or tarmac. Roads of this kind were known as flexible pavements.

By the early nineteenth century – the start of the railway age – men such as John McAdam and Thomas Telford had created a British road network totalling some 200,000 km, of which about one sixth was privately owned toll roads called turnpikes. In the first half of the nineteenth century, many roads in the US were built to the new standards, of which the National Pike from West Virginia to Illinois was perhaps the most notable.

In the twentieth century, the ever-increasing use of motor vehicles threatened to break up roads built to nineteenth-century standards, so new techniques had to be developed.

On routes with heavy traffic, flexible pavements were replaced by rigid pavements, in which the top layer was concrete, 15 to 30 centimetres thick, laid on a prepared bed. Nowadays steel bars are laid within the concrete. This not only restrains shrinkage during setting, but also reduces expansion in warm weather. As a result, it is possible to lay long slabs without danger of cracking.

The demands of heavy traffic led to the concept of high-speed, long-distance roads, with access – or slip-lanes – spaced widely apart. The US Bronx River Parkway of 1925 was followed by several variants – Germany's autobahns and the Pan American Highway. Such roads – especially the intercity autobahns with their separate multi-lane carriageways for each direction – were the predecessors of today's motorways.

Bridges

The development by the Romans of the arched bridge marked the beginning of scientific bridge-building; hitherto, bridges had generally been crossings in the form of felled trees or flat stone blocks. Absorbing the load by compression, arched bridges are very strong. Most were built of stone, but brick and timber were also used. A fine early example is at Alcantara in Spain, built of granite by the Romans in AD 105 to span the River Tagus. In modern times, metal and concrete arched bridges have been constructed. The first significant metal bridge, built of cast iron in 1779, still stands at Ironbridge in England.

Steel, with its superior strength-to-weight ratio, soon replaced iron in metal bridge-work. In the railway age, the truss (or girder) bridge became popular. Built of wood or metal, the truss beam consists of upper and lower horizontal booms joined by vertical or inclined members.

The suspension bridge has a deck supported by suspenders that drop from one or more overhead cables. It requires strong anchorage at each end to resist the inward tension of the cables, and the deck is strengthened to control distortion by moving loads or high winds. Such bridges are nevertheless light, and therefore the most suitable for very long spans. The Clifton Suspension Bridge in the UK, designed by Isambard Kingdom Brunel (1806–59) to span the Avon Gorge in England, is famous both for its beautiful setting and for its elegant design. The 1998 Akashi Kaikyo Bridge in Japan has a span of 1,991 metres, which is the longest to date.

Cantilever bridges, such as the 1889 Forth Rail Bridge in Scotland, exploit the potential of steel construction to produce a wide clearwater space. The spans have a central supporting pier and meet midstream. The downward thrust, where the spans meet, is countered by firm anchorage of the spans at their other ends. Although the suspension bridge can span a wider gap, the cantilever is relatively stable, and this was important for nineteenth-century railway builders. The world's longest cantilever span – 549 metres – is that of the Quebec rail bridge in Canada, constructed in 1918.

Questions 1–3

Label the diagram below.

*Choose **NO MORE THAN TWO WORDS AND/OR A NUMBER** from the passage for each answer.*

Flexible Pavement

Surface layer

Middle layer
(2... deep)

Foundation

Tarmacadam (1... and stone chips)

Crushed stone
dust and 3...

Questions 4–7

Do the following statements agree with the information given in Reading Passage 1?

Write

TRUE   *if the statement agrees with the information*
FALSE   *if the statement contradicts the information*
NOT GIVEN *if there is no information on this*

4   Road construction improved continuously between the first and eighteenth centuries.

5   In Britain, during the nineteenth century, only the very rich could afford to use toll roads.

6   Nineteenth-century road surfaces were inadequate for heavy motor traffic.

7   Traffic speeds on long-distance highways were unregulated in the early part of the twentieth century.

Questions 8–13

Complete the table below.

Use **ONE WORD ONLY** from the passage for each answer.

Type of bridge	Features	Example(s)
Arched bridge	• Introduced by the **8** .... • Very strong. • Usually made of **9**	Alcantara, Spain Ironbridge, UK
Truss bridge	• Made of wood or metal. • Popular for railways.	
Suspension bridge	• Has a suspended deck. • Strong but **10**	Clifton, UK Akashi Kaikyo, Japan (currently the **11** .... span)
Cantilever bridge	• Made of **12** .... • More **13** .... than the suspension bridge.	Quebec, Canada

Neanderthals and modern humans

A The evolutionary processes that have made modern humans so different from other animals are hard to determine without an ability to examine human species that have not achieved similar things. However, in a scientific masterpiece, Svante Paabo and his colleagues from the Max Planck Institute for Evolutionary Anthropology, in Leipzig, have made such a comparison possible. In 2009, at a meeting of the American Association for the Advancement of Science, they made public an analysis of the genome* of Neanderthal man.

B *Homo neanderthalensis*, to give its proper name, lived in Europe and parts of Asia from 400,000 years ago to 30,000 years ago. Towards the end of this period it shared its range with interlopers in the form of *Homo sapiens***, who were spreading out from Africa. However, the two species did not settle down to a stable cohabitation. For reasons which are as yet unknown, the arrival of *Homo sapiens* in a region was always quickly followed by the disappearance of Neanderthals.

C Before 2009, Dr Paabo and his team had conducted only a superficial comparison between the DNA of Neanderthals and modern humans. Since then, they have performed a more thorough study and, in doing so, have shed a fascinating light on the intertwined history of the two species. That history turns out to be more intertwined than many had previously believed.

D Dr Paabo and his colleagues compared their Neanderthal genome (painstakingly reconstructed from three bone samples collected from a cave in Croatia) with that of five living humans from various parts of Africa and Eurasia. Previous genetic analysis, which had only examined DNA passed from mother to child in cellular structures called mitochondria, had suggested no interbreeding between Neanderthals and modern humans. The new, more extensive examination, which looks at DNA in the cell nucleus rather than in the mitochondria, shows this conclusion is wrong. By comparing the DNA in the cell nucleus of Africans (whose ancestors could not have crossbred with Neanderthals, since they did not overlap with them) and various Eurasians (whose ancestors could have crossbred with Neanderthals), Dr Paabo has shown that Eurasians are between one percent and four percent Neanderthal.

E That is intriguing. It shows that even after several hundred thousand years of separation, the two species were inter-fertile. It is strange, though, that no Neanderthal mitochondrial DNA has turned up in modern humans, since the usual pattern of invasion in historical times was for the invaders' males to mate with the invaded's females. One piece of self-knowledge, then – at least for non-Africans – is that they have a dash of Neanderthal in them. But Dr Paabo's work also illuminates the differences between the species. By comparing modern humans, Neanderthals, and chimpanzees, it is possible to distinguish genetic changes which are shared by several species of human in their evolution away from the great-ape lineage, from those which are unique to *Homo sapiens*.

F More than 90 percent of the 'human accelerated regions'*** that have been identified in modern people are found in Neanderthals too. However, the rest are not. Dr Paabo has identified 212 parts of the genome that seem to have undergone significant evolution since the species split. The state of genome science is still quite primitive, and it is often unclear what any given bit of DNA is actually doing. But an examination of the 20 largest regions of DNA that have evolved in this way shows that they include several genes which are associated with cognitive ability, and whose malfunction causes serious mental problems. These genes therefore look like good places to start the search for modern humanity's essence.

G The newly evolved regions of DNA also include a gene called RUNX2, which controls bone growth. That may account for differences in the shape of the skull and the rib cage between the two species. By contrast an earlier phase of the study had already shown that Neanderthals and moderns share the same version of a gene called FOXP2, which is involved in the ability to speak, and which differs in chimpanzees. It is all, then, very promising – and a second coup in quick succession for Dr Paabo. Another of his teams has revealed the existence of a hitherto unsuspected species of human, using mitochondrial DNA found in a little-finger bone. If that species, too, could have its full genome read, humanity's ability to know itself would be enhanced even further.

---

*   an individual's complete set of genes

**   the scientific name for modern humans

***   parts of the human brain which evolved very rapidly

Questions 14–26

Questions 14–18

Look at the following characteristics (Questions 14–18) and the list of species below.

*Match each feature with the correct species, **A**, **B** or **C**.*

*Write the correct letter, **A**, **B** or **C**.*

NB You may use any letter more than once.

14 Once lived in Europe and Asia.

15 Originated in Africa.

16 Did not survive long after the arrival of immigrants.

17 Interbred with another species.

18 Appears not to have passed on mitochondrial DNA to another species.

List of species

A *Homo neanderthalensis*

B *Homo sapiens*

C both *Homo neanderthalensis* and *Homo sapiens*

Questions 19–23

*Reading Passage 2 has seven paragraphs, **A–G**.*

Which paragraph contains the following information?

*Write the correct letter, **A–G**.*

19 an account of the rejection of a theory

20 reference to an unexplained link between two events

21 the identification of a skill-related gene common to both Neanderthals and modern humans

22 the announcement of a scientific breakthrough

23 an interesting gap in existing knowledge

Questions 24–26

Complete the summary below.

*Choose **NO MORE THAN THREE WORDS** from the passage for each answer.*

The nature of modern humans

Recent work in the field of evolutionary anthropology has made it possible to compare modern humans with other related species. Genetic analysis resulted in several new findings. First, despite the length of time for which *Homo sapiens* and *Homo neanderthalensis* had developed separately, **24**.................. did take place. Secondly, genes which evolved after modern humans split from Neanderthals are connected with cognitive ability and skeletal **25**.................. .

The potential for this line of research to shed light on the nature of modern humans was further strengthened when analysis of a **26**.................. led to the discovery of a new human species.

The Future of fish

The face of the ocean has changed completely since the first commercial fishers cast their nets and hooks over a thousand years ago. Fisheries intensified over the centuries, but even by the nineteenth century it was still felt, justifiably, that the plentiful resources of the sea were for the most part beyond the reach of fishing, and so there was little need to restrict fishing or create protected areas. The twentieth century heralded an escalation in fishing intensity that is unprecedented in the history of the oceans, and modern fishing technologies leave fish no place to hide. Today, the only refuges from fishing are those we deliberately create. Unhappily, the sea trails far behind the land in terms of the area and the quality of protection given.

For centuries, as fishing and commerce have expanded, we have held onto the notion that the sea is different from the land. We still view it as a place where people and nations should be free to come and go at will, as well as somewhere that should be free for us to exploit. Perhaps this is why we have been so reluctant to protect the sea. On land, protected areas have proliferated as human populations have grown. Here, compared to the sea, we have made greater headway in our struggle to maintain the richness and variety of wildlife and landscape. Twelve percent of the world's land is now contained in protected areas, whereas the corresponding figure for the sea is but three-fifths of one percent. Worse still, most marine protected areas allow some fishing to continue. Areas off-limits to all exploitation cover something like one five-thousandth of the total area of the world's seas.

Today, we are belatedly coming to realise that 'natural refuges' from fishing have played a critical role in sustaining fisheries, and maintaining healthy and diverse marine ecosystems. This does not mean that marine reserves can rebuild fisheries on their own – other management measures are also required for that. However, places that are off-limits to fishing constitute the last and most important part of our package of reform for fisheries management. They underpin and enhance all our other efforts. There are limits to protection though.

Reserves cannot bring back what has died out. We can never resurrect globally extinct species, and restoring locally extinct animals may require reintroductions from elsewhere, if natural dispersal from remaining populations is insufficient. We are also seeing, in cases such as northern cod in Canada, that fishing can shift marine ecosystems into different states, where different mixes of species prevail. In many cases, these species are less desirable, since the prime fishing targets have gone or are much reduced in numbers, and changes may be difficult to reverse, even with a complete moratorium on fishing. The Mediterranean sailed by Ulysses, the legendary king of ancient Greece, supported abundant monk seals, loggerhead turtles and porpoises. Their disappearance through hunting and overfishing has totally restructured food webs, and recovery is likely to be much harder to achieve than their destruction was. This means that the sooner we act to protect marine life, the more certain will be our success.

To some people, creating marine reserves is an admission of failure. According to their logic, reserves should not be necessary if we have done our work properly in managing the uses we make of the sea. Many fisheries managers are still wedded to the idea that one day their models will work, and politicians will listen to their advice. Just give the approach time, and success will be theirs. How much time have we got? This approach has been tried and refined for the last 50 years. There have been few successes with which to feather the managers' caps, but a growing litany of failure. The Common Fisheries Policy, the European Union's instrument for the management of fisheries and aquaculture, exemplifies the worst pitfalls: flawed models, flawed advice, watered-down recommendations from government bureaucrats and then the disregard of much of this advice by politicians. When it all went wrong, as it inevitably had to, Europe sent its boats to other countries in order to obtain fish for far less than they were actually worth.

We are squandering the wealth of oceans. If we don't break out of this cycle of failure, humanity will lose a key source of protein, and much more besides. Disrupting natural ecosystem processes, such as water purification, nutrient cycling, and carbon storage, could have ramifications for human life itself. We can go a long way to avoiding this catastrophic mistake with simple common sense management. Marine reserves lie at the heart of the reform. But they will not be sufficient if they are implemented only here and there to shore up the crumbling edifice of the 'rational fisheries management' envisioned by scientists in the 1940s and 1950s. They have to be placed centre stage as a fundamental underpinning for everything we do in the oceans. Reserves are a first resort, not a final resort when all else fails.

Questions 27–40

Questions 27–31

Do the following statements agree with the views of the writer in Reading Passage 3?

Write

YES	if the statement agrees with the claims of the writer
NO	if the statement contradicts the claims of the writer
NOT GIVEN	if it is impossible to say what the writer thinks about this

27 It is more than a thousand years since people started to catch fish for commercial use.

28 In general, open access to the oceans is still regarded as desirable.

29 Sea fishing is now completely banned in the majority of protected areas.

30 People should be encouraged to reduce the amount of fish they eat.

31 The re-introduction of certain mammals to the Mediterranean is a straightforward task.

Questions 32–34

Choose the correct letter, **A**, **B**, **C** or **D**.

32 What does the writer mean with the question, 'How much time have we got?' in the fifth paragraph?

    A Fisheries policies are currently based on uncertain estimates.

    B Accurate predictions will allow governments to plan properly.

    C Fisheries managers should provide clearer information.

    D Action to protect fish stocks is urgently needed.

33 What is the writer's comment on the Common Fisheries Policy?

    A Measures that it advocated were hastily implemented.

    B Officials exaggerated some of its recommendations.

    C It was based on predictions which were inaccurate.

    D The policy makers acquired a good reputation.

34 What is the writer's conclusion concerning the decline of marine resources?

    A The means of avoiding the worst outcomes needs to be prioritised.

    B Measures already taken to avoid a crisis are probably sufficient.

    C The situation is now so severe that there is no likely solution.

    D It is no longer clear which measures would be most effective.

Questions 35–40

*Complete the summary using the list of words/phrases, **A–J**, below.*

Measures to protect the oceans

Up till the twentieth century the world's supply of fish was sufficient for its needs. It was unnecessary to introduce **35** ……………… of any kind, because large areas of the oceans were inaccessible. However, as **36** ……………… improved, this situation changed, and in the middle of the twentieth century, policies were introduced to regulate **37** ……………… .

These policies have not succeeded. Today, by comparison with **38** ……………… , the oceans have very little legal protection.

Despite the doubts that many officials have about the concept of **39** ……………… , these should be at the heart of any action taken. The consequences of further **40** ……………… are very serious, and may even affect our continuing existence.

A action	**B** controls	**C** failure	**D** fish catches
E fish processing	**F** fishing techniques	**G** large boats	
H marine reserves	**I** the land	**J** the past	

Writing module (1 hour)

WRITING TASK 1 You should spend about 20 minutes on this task.

> **The charts below show the percentage of time younger and older people spend on various Internet activities in their free time (excluding email).**
>
> **Summarise the information by selecting and reporting the main features, and make comparisons where relevant.**

Write at least 150 words.

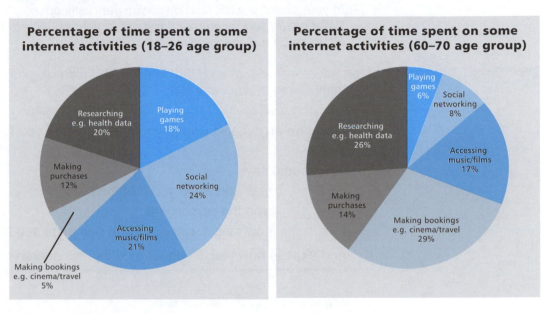

WRITING TASK 2 You should spend about 40 minutes on this task.

Write about the following topic:

> **Some people feel that the legal age at which people can marry should be at least 21.**
>
> **To what extent do you agree or disagree?**

Give reasons for your answer and include any relevant examples from your own knowledge and experience.

Write at least 250 words.

Speaking module (11–14 minutes)

Answer these questions.

Tell me about your country.

Which part of the country are you from?
Has your family always lived there?
Do you like living in your country? Why/Why not?
Is your country changing a lot? How?

Let's talk about shops.

Do you enjoy going shopping? Why?
In your country, what time do shops generally open?
What would you recommend visitors to your country to buy? Why?
How are shops changing in your country? Why?

PART 2 You have one minute to make notes on the following topic. Then you have up to two minutes to talk about it.

> Describe an occasion when you met someone you hadn't seen for several years.
>
> You should say:
>
> > how and when you met the person
> >
> > who the person was
> >
> > how long it was since you had last seen him/her
>
> and explain how you felt about meeting this person again.

Did you recognise him/her straight away?
Had he/she changed a lot?

PART 3 Consider these questions and then answer them.

Now let's talk about keeping in contact with people we know.

In what different ways can people keep in touch with each other?
How important do you think it is to keep in touch with friends? Why/Why not?
Which way of keeping in touch do you think is most popular with young people?

Now let's consider the ways in which people change as they grow older.

What are the reasons why people change as they grow older?
Why do you think some people change more than others?
At about what age do you think people change the most? Why/Why not?

Now let's discuss long-term relationships.

How valuable do you think long-term friendships are compared with new relationships? Why/Why not?
Do you agree that maintaining long-term relationships sometimes requires effort? Why/Why not?

GENERAL TRAINING TEST

Reading module (1 hour)

Guidance

Overview

The General Training Reading test contains three sections, and lasts for one hour, so you have twenty minutes to do each section. The first and second parts of the test are generally easier than the third, so you might decide to spend less time on these. You can make notes on the question paper, but all your answers have to be written on a separate mark sheet, so you must allow enough time to do this. The test has a total of 40 questions, so in two of the sections there are 13 questions, and in one there are 14 questions.

The first section of the test consists of two texts about some aspect of everyday life. Topics are varied and might include accommodation, travel, leisure, entertainment or driving. Each of the texts is approximately 300–350 words in total.

The second section contains two texts about some aspect of work or training. Again, topics are varied, and could include careers, jobs, qualifications, health and safety, salary and benefits. Each of the texts is between 350 and 400 words in length.

The third section has only one text of about 850–900 words, and is about any subject of general interest. Topics might include geography, history, science, nature or sport, but the texts will be generally accessible to readers of any background.

Tasks

The General Training Reading paper uses a variety of task types, including:
- Giving short answers to questions.
- Deciding whether statements/opinions correspond to what is written in a reading passage.
- Matching statements to people or events which are mentioned in a reading passage.
- Completing a summary, or individual sentences based on a reading passage.
- Completing a table, a diagram, a flow chart, or notes based on a reading passage.
- Choosing a statement about a reading passage from several options.
- Choosing the answer to a question about a reading passage from several options.
- Choosing the best heading for each of the paragraphs in a reading passage.

In some tasks you will have to write words or phrases, and in other tasks you will have to write letters or numbers.

Focus

The testing focus of the General Training test is similar to that of the Academic Training test. See page 39 for more information.

Preparation Tips and Strategies

You can use the same preparation tips and strategies for the General Reading test as you can for the Academic Reading test. See page 39 for more information.

CREATIVE TOYS

A

Bath time animals

Five foam mix-and-match animal jigsaws. Pieces stick easily to damp tiles and ceramic surfaces. A great product for keeping young children entertained in the bath. Assembled animals approximately 16 cm.

B

Chef's outfit

Young children will love to play at being a master chef in this cute costume of apron, floppy hat and oven glove. With convenient Velcro fastenings, this set is suitable for a broad range of sizes. Available in two colours: blue and red – please specify your preference.

C

Chimalong

An excellent choice, even for the very young. This small xylophone has eight chimes, and is accompanied by a book, with instructions for playing twelve familiar tunes. The chimes and instructions are colour-coded, making it easy for children to learn how to play the tunes.

D

Carpenter's tools

This fantastic junior tool box is great for all young children who want to copy adults and do some real woodworking. The set includes: a tool box, hammer, saw, mallet, chisel, spanners, sandpaper, screwdrivers and pliers – everything needed to tackle simple projects. *NB: Not suitable for children under eight years. Needs adult supervision.*

E

Cardboard playhouse

A unique playhouse providing hours of fun and imaginative play for young children. It is constructed in durable cardboard and is 100 percent recyclable! It is easy to assemble, and can be folded flat or used as extra storage when not in use. Pink, blue, green, silver or brown – please state preference. Overall size 90 x 67.5 x 128 centimetres. *NB: This item is not available for overseas delivery or our gift-wrapping service.*

F

Doll-making kit

A great creative kit for making an adorable ballerina doll. Children can give her a name and make it official with the birth certificate which is included! No pins or needles required. Contains one soft doll body, wool, lace, ribbon, adhesive tape, coloured pencils, birth certificate and detailed instructions. *NB: Not suitable for children under five years.*

Questions 1–7

Questions 1–7

Look at the six advertisements for toys, **A–F** on page 154.

For which toy are the following statements true?

Write the correct letter, **A–F**, in boxes 1–7 on your answer sheet.

NB: You may use any letter more than once.

1 There is a range of colours to choose from.

2 The size of this can be adjusted to suit the child.

3 This cannot be sent to addresses in other countries.

4 Children can use this to make things out of wood.

5 Water will not damage this toy.

6 This contains the parts needed to make a toy.

7 This is a type of musical instrument.

Tip strip

Questions 1–7

- The statements *don't* follow the order of information in the texts.
- You *may* not use *all* of the letters for your answers. You *may* use one or more letter *more than once*.
- For each statement, find any texts which contain words or phrases with similar meanings (there may be more than one), and then decide which text matches the statement.
- When you are writing your answer, *don't* copy the words. Only write the *letter* of the correct answer.

Question 1

Find all the advertisements that mention colour. Choose the one that mentions 'a range' of (several) colours.

Question 2

First find all the advertisements which mention size. Choose the advertisement that mentions being able to *change* the size.

Question 5

Find the advertisement containing words related to 'water'. There is only one.

Tip strip

Questions 8–14

- The statements are in the same order as the information in the letter.
- Some of the words in the statements might be the same or similar to words in the letter. This *doesn't* mean that the statement must be true.
- Read the *whole* statement carefully before you decide whether it matches information in the letter or not.
- For your answer, write *T* or *F* or *NG*. *Don't* write complete words.

Question 8

To find where the answer is, look for a word which has a similar meaning to 'managed'. Then read the sentence carefully.

Question 10

To find where the answer is, look for the place where prices and breakfast are mentioned. Then read the sentence carefully.

Question 12

Find a word which is related in meaning to 'arrival'. Then check what the letter says about the 'earliest' time guests can arrive.

Dear Mr and Mrs Burton,

Thank you for booking your stay with us at the Loch Cullen Hotel, one of Scotland's best-known and oldest family-run hotels.

We are delighted to confirm your reservation from 16 June to 20 June. Unfortunately, the double room you requested is not available, and we only have single or twin rooms to offer during that period. We have reserved a twin room for you, but please let us know if you would prefer two singles.

The rate will be £55.00 per person per night, which includes a full Scottish breakfast and tax. We are currently offering a special rate for Sunday nights – £25 per person – please contact us as soon as possible if you wish to extend your stay and take up this offer.

Check-in is from 2 p.m. and check-out is 11 a.m. on the morning of your departure. If for any reason you require a different time then please let us know in advance and we'll do our best to help you.

The Loch Cullen Hotel has a choice of two distinctly different dining experiences. Choose either the Lounge Bar where you'll find freshly produced light meals, or the Loch Restaurant for more formal dining, but with a relaxed atmosphere. We can offer you a range of locally-sourced food, such as our award-winning haggis or Scottish smoked salmon. Throughout the hotel we use the very best fresh Scottish produce.

On departure, guests can settle their bill in cash, or by cheque, debit card or credit card. Thank you for guaranteeing your booking with a credit card number, which will only be used in the event of a late cancellation. If cancelled up to 24 hours before the day of arrival no fee will be charged. If cancelled later, or in the case that a guest doesn't arrive, then the first night will be charged in full.

If you have any questions about your reservation or the hotel, please don't hesitate to contact us. We look forward to welcoming you on your arrival.

Yours sincerely,

Sarah Peterson (Manager)

Questions 8–14

Do the following statements agree with the information given in the text above?

Write

TRUE	*if the statement agrees with the information*
FALSE	*if the statement contradicts the information*
NOT GIVEN	*if there is no information on this*

8 The Loch Cullen Hotel is managed by an international company.

9 One room with two beds has been reserved.

10 Prices will be reduced for guests who do not require breakfast.

11 There is a temporary price reduction for Sunday-night stays.

12 The earliest time of arrival at the hotel is normally 2 p.m.

13 Dinner in the Loch Restaurant must be booked in advance.

14 If less than 24 hours' notice of cancellation is given, there is no charge.

Minnesota Department of Natural Resources (DNR)

Volunteering program

Volunteers work with DNR managers, professionals and technicians to help manage the state's diverse natural resources. Volunteer positions range from jobs requiring no previous experience to specialist positions requiring extensive skill and experience. Volunteers provide work which supplements DNR personnel. Volunteers help to preserve and enhance Minnesota's natural beauty for the enjoyment of people of all ages, interests and abilities.

Follow these steps to sign up as a volunteer for DNR:

Volunteer opportunities are available throughout the state at State Parks, State Forest Campgrounds, Wildlife Management Areas, fisheries and hatcheries, the 150+ DNR area offices, four regional headquarter offices, the St. Paul Central Office and at special event sites. Check our website to learn about volunteer positions available in your area.

Contact the DNR officer who is designated for the project you are interested in. (If you live in Greater Minnesota, you may use our toll free number at 1-555 646-6367. Hearing impaired individuals may call (651) 296-5484. The DNR officer will inform you if the position is still open and will register you.

Arrive on time (or a little early) to work on the project for which you registered to work. The schedule you agree to is important: be sure to call if you will be absent or need to leave early. The DNR is counting on you to be a dependable volunteer.

While working for the DNR, take account of the following guidelines:

- Represent the DNR in a positive fashion. You are not expected to be knowledgeable in all areas concerning the DNR. If working with the public in your volunteer position, all questions from them related to DNR policies and procedures are to be passed on to your supervisor, or to the DNR Information Line at 1-888-646-6367. Avoid expressing a personal opinion.

- Keep a note of your hours. This is important for liability coverage, for reporting to the legislature, and for volunteer recognition. When the project is finished, turn in your records to your supervisor, who will pass them on to the programme manager.

- Your supervisor will be happy to discuss any worries that you may have, as well as any special needs, and try to offer solutions that may help you perform your volunteer duties better.

Questions 15–27

Questions 15–21

Complete the flow chart below.

Choose **ONE WORD ONLY** from the text for each answer.

Volunteering for the DNR

Find out about local vacancies from the DNR's **15** ....

↓

Get in touch with the named DNR **16** ....

↓

Register for the post.

↓

Turn up punctually for work (call if you need to change your **17** ....).

↓ ↓ ↓

Refer questions about the DNR from the **18** .... to your supervisor (do not give your own **19** ....).

Give a record of your **20** .... to your supervisor.

Tell your supervisor if you have any concerns or particular **21** ....

Top tips on how to get further up the career ladder

Moving jobs is no longer quite as easy as it was just a couple of years ago, prompting many to look to develop their careers within existing companies until the recruitment outlook improves.

The following tips can help you take control of your career and make yourself more attractive to both your current and any future employer:

- Keep up with industry developments

  Ensuring you are up-to-date with the latest trends in your industry through attending conferences can make you an invaluable employee, and change the way managers see you, says John Grange, an adviser at free business advice and support service *Business Link.*

  In recent years, online networking, using corporate sites such as *LinkedIn*, has also given employees the ability to liaise with people doing similar work. It's a great way of keeping up-to-date with what people in similar jobs and industries are thinking about, and plenty of people are willing to help if you have a problem or want some advice.

  But Leon Benjamin, author of the book *Winning By Sharing*, warns that the effectiveness of such sites in advancing your career varies considerably, depending on your industry sector 'For people who're working in digital media it's everything, but in the building trade it's almost pointless because of its low level of take up,' he says.

- Request suitable training

  Ensuring you have access to training to improve your skills is essential to progressing both your career and earning potential. By getting the right skills, individuals can sometimes get salary increases, as well as making themselves more likely to gain promotion.

  Finding the right type of training, though, is vital. Apart from on-the-job training, there are self-help books that can be found in book shops or libraries, as well as formal courses. Individuals should decide what their genuine areas of weakness are, and then talk about them with their Staff Development coordinator to find out what kind of training might be best.

- Broaden your experience

  Experiencing other parts of the business through temporary roles or job-shadowing can give you a more rounded view of the organisation and ensure you won't be pigeon-holed in one particular area.

Grange says, 'If you have an appreciation of what goes on within all departments you become much more valuable to the business, because you understand that if you take an action over here, there's a knock-on effect over there.'

- Work with your manager

One of the key skills is dealing with your boss, and part of that is knowing what your boss is being judged by. They all have targets, from the chief executive and other more senior managers, so look at ways in which you can help them to deliver those while still helping yourself.

Look at the top tips in the passage above.

Complete the notes below.

*Choose **NO MORE THAN TWO WORDS** from the text for each answer.*

Keep up with developments by:

- going to conferences

- **22** .... , using business websites (but not useful for employees in the **23** ....)

Ask for training

- could result in a salary increase

- types of training – on-the-job, books or **24** ....

- identify weaknesses and discuss them with the person in charge of **25** ....

Get more experience by:

- doing temporary work in other departments

- **26** ....

Work with the manager

- find out what their **27** .... are and help them succeed

---

Tip strip

Questions 22–27

- Notes *might not* follow the order of the text *exactly*, but the headings will help you to find the right places in the text.

- Write *either* one word *or* two words for your answers. *Don't* write more than this.

- Your answers should fit the spaces grammatically as well as in meaning.

- *Don't* change any words. Write your answers exactly as they appear in the text.

Question 22

This is the second part of a list of *two* things. Find what the second thing is by looking for 'also' in the text, then reading the sentence carefully.

Question 24

To find the place where the answer is, look for the part in the text about training.

The answer is one of *three* types of training. Find where the text mentions the other two types, and then look for the third type.

Question 27

The notes have 'their' in front of the space, and 'are' after the space, so the answer is a plural noun phrase.

The Spotted Flycatcher

A

Despite its rather dull plumage and less than impressive vocal repertoire, the Spotted Flycatcher has always attracted a great deal of public attention in Britain. However, the bird is resident here for only a small part of the year. Although one of the last summer visitors to arrive, it begins to move south in late July, heading through western France and Iberia from August to October, and reaching North Africa in September. Recoveries of birds that have been ringed suggest that many winter in coastal West Africa, but others continue south to cross the Equator. Just how far south the birds winter is unclear; one juvenile ringed in Wales during August (which could have been on passage from a breeding area outside Britain) was recovered in South Africa the following March.

B

In the eighteenth century, Gilbert White, one of the first English naturalists to make careful observations of his surroundings and record these in a systematic way, commented that the annual return of 'his' Spotted Flycatchers occurred almost exactly to the day. An examination of his journals confirms this consistency in arrival dates, with a concentration of sightings around 20 May each year. Records logged through a British Trust for Ornithology (BTO)-led project show that the pattern of arrival still delivers the bulk of Spotted Flycatchers to Britain in the second half of May, though average arrival dates may now be slightly earlier than they were during White's time.

C

Most Spotted Flycatcher nests are built against a vertical surface, such as a wall, but some may be positioned on a beam, and very occasionally, the species will make use of a hole. Although both sexes get involved in building the nest, it is the female who does most of the work. The nest itself is a fairly delicate structure, slightly built and containing moss, wool, hair and cobwebs. The female will deposit four or five eggs or, rarely, six, into this before she initiates incubation – a job that she undertakes almost entirely on her own. Bouts of incubation are broken by short periods of seven to ten minutes, when the female may leave the nest to feed. While she is away the male will appear, typically as if from nowhere, to watch the nest, very occasionally even settling on the eggs.

D

Once the eggs hatch, the female will continue to brood them until they are seven to ten days old; the young are blind and naked through to day five. Both sexes will then provide food for the growing chicks, sometimes bringing them through to successful fledging, and avoiding the unwelcome attentions of nest predators like cats. Newly fledged young are fairly conspicuous; noisily, they continue to beg for food from their parents for at least another 10-12 days. The pair may then initiate another breeding attempt, sometimes in the same nest. There are records of young from the first brood attending and feeding young from the second brood, a behaviour that also occurs in a number of other bird species.

E

Over the main period of egg production females take more calcium-rich prey (like small snails and woodlice). If a second batch of eggs is laid, the number of eggs is reduced to three or four, probably reflecting a reduction in the availability of insect prey later in the season. Research has shown that on cold days (or in the cool of early morning) the Spotted Flycatcher switches from taking larger, aerial insect prey to gleaning smaller prey from amongst foliage. These smaller prey are likely to be less nutritious, and a run of cooler days late in the breeding season may reduce the chances of the birds successfully rearing a second brood.

F

The Spotted Flycatcher lacks the more brightly marked plumage of many other birds, and the lack of easily recognisable features means it can be mistaken for another, equally drab species, such as the Dunnock, or even the female House Sparrow. Fortunately, the Spotted Flycatcher can also be identified from its behaviour. Spotted Flycatchers are seldom seen on the ground, but usually feed from a perch, making sallies after aerial insects. The flycatcher often adopts an upright posture when perching, making the bird appear rather sleek. Additionally, it is rare to see several Spotted

Flycatchers together unless they happen to be a family of two adults feeding newly-fledged young (the latter looking very different from their parents because of their strongly patterned plumage). One other feature is the audible snapping sound that the bill sometimes makes when the bird snatches an insect from the air.

G

Data from the BTO show an 86 percent downturn in the breeding population of Spotted Flycatchers over the period 1967–2006, a pattern seemingly repeated elsewhere in Europe, where numbers are estimated to have fallen by 59 percent since 1980. However, ongoing and planned work should help to reveal the underlying causes of this trend. In particular, the BTO has a project to analyse nest data already collected. Work will need to be carried out elsewhere as well, looking at the Spotted Flycatcher in its wintering grounds. Understanding the factors that drive Spotted Flycatcher numbers should stimulate conservation action and help to secure the future of this bird.

Tip strip

Questions 28–34

- The headings are *not* in the same order as the information in the text.
- You can only use each heading once.
- Read all the headings quickly before you read the text.
- If you have chosen one of the headings for a paragraph near the beginning, and then find that it fits a later paragraph better, check your answers.
- Don't choose a heading just because it contains words from the text. A heading should be about the *whole* paragraph.

Question 29

Paragraph B mentions 'sightings', so read this paragraph quickly to see if 'regularity' is one of the main themes.

Question 32

Only three of the paragraphs mention food or feeding (C, D and E). *One* of these describes what the birds eat in some detail. Read this paragraph and check that it mentions different times of the year.

Question 34

Look for a paragraph containing the idea of 'decline' or fall. There is only one.

Check whether this paragraph refers to 'reversing' (completely changing) the decline.

Questions 28–40

Questions 28–34

The text above has **SEVEN** paragraphs, **A–G**.

Choose the correct heading, *i–ix*, from the list of headings below.

Write the correct number, *i–ix*.

List of Headings

i	A breeding partnership
ii	Danger from predators
iii	Geographic range
iv	Seasonal changes in diet
v	The regularity of first sightings
vi	A lack of accurate data
vii	Reversing the decline
viii	Rearing the young
ix	Physical features

28 Paragraph **A**   ....

29 Paragraph **B**   ....

30 Paragraph **C**   ....

31 Paragraph **D**   ....

32 Paragraph **E**   ....

33 Paragraph **F**   ....

34 Paragraph **G**   ....

Questions 35–38

Complete the summary below.

Choose **NO MORE THAN TWO WORDS** from the text for each answer.

Tip strip

Question 35

Look for a word in the text with a similar meaning to 'feathers'.

The word before the space is 'quite', so the answer is an adjective or an adverb.

Question 37

'A' comes before the space, so the answer is a singular noun phrase.

Identifying the Spotted Flycatcher

The Spotted Flycatcher can be hard to identify, as its singing is unremarkable, and its feathers are quite **35** .... It can best be distinguished by its behaviour.

The Spotted Flycatcher usually waits for its prey on a **36** .... It is normally seen alone, or as part of a **37** .... Finally, when it catches prey it often produces a **38** ....

Questions 39 to 40.

Choose the correct letter, **A**, **B**, **C** or **D**.

39 What does the writer say about the seasonal movements of Spotted Flycatchers?

    A They can be found in Britain throughout most of the year.

    B Their time of arrival in Britain has changed considerably since the eighteenth century.

    C Ringing them has only provided evidence of their routes within Europe.

    D Some of them migrate between the northern and southern hemispheres.

40 The nests of Spotted Flycatchers

    A have to be sturdily built.

    B may be used for more than one brood.

    C are normally constructed by the male.

    D must hold up to ten eggs at a time.

Tip strip

Questions 39–40

- The questions follow the order of information in the text.
- The four options *may not* follow the order of information in the text.
- After you've chosen an answer, check that the other options are wrong.
- It's better to guess than to leave a question unanswered.

Question 40

Information about the birds' nests is contained in Paragraph C and Paragraph D. So to be sure of the correct answer, you have to read *both* these paragraphs.

Writing module (1 hour)

Guidance

Overview

The General Training Writing test lasts for an hour and consists of two parts. The first part is shorter than the second, and carries only one third of the marks, so you should spend about 20 minutes on this part and 40 minutes on the second part.

For each part you should allow enough time to plan what you are going to say before you begin writing, and to check what you have written afterwards.

Tasks

Task 1

In the first part, you have to write a letter with a minimum of 150 words altogether, in response to a situation which is described in the task. The situation might be related to social life, or it might be related to work life, and it might be a letter to a friend or a letter to an official or a work colleague.

You are provided with a list of three things which your letter should include.

You have to write in an appropriate style according to the situation.

Task 2

In the second part you have to write an essay with a minimum of 250 words. This involves giving your own opinion about a situation or point of view which is described in the task. Topics are varied, and might include health, lifestyles, environment, or education, but you do not have to have any special knowledge to be able to do the task.

Focus

The testing focus for the General Training Writing test is similar to that of the Academic Writing test. See page 52 for more information.

Preparation Tips and Strategies

As you cannot predict what the topics of the General Training Writing test will be, you should read about different topics using a wide variety of sources, such as magazines, newspapers, letters, leaflets, advertisements and websites.

At the same time, you should practise writing both letters and essays to a time limit.

You should spend about 20 minutes on this task.

> **You want something that you can't buy in your own country. You decide to ask an English friend to help you.**
>
> **Write a letter to the friend. In your letter**
>
> - **say what you want,**
>
> - **explain why you want it,**
>
> - **suggest how the friend could help.**

Write at least 150 words.

You do not need to write any addresses.

Begin your letter as follows:

   Dear ……………… ,

You should spend about 40 minutes on this task.

Write about the following topic:

> **Some people think that there are now too many cars on the roads, and that they are spoiling our towns and cities.**
>
> **Do you agree or disagree?**

Give reasons for your answer, and include any relevant examples from your own knowledge or experience.

Write at least 250 words.

SPEAKING FILE

In the first part of the speaking test, the examiner will ask you questions about yourself and about things you are familiar with.

Watch the full test on your DVD.

Tips

- Listen very carefully to the question so that your reply is relevant.
- If you don't understand the question, ask the examiner to repeat it, or tell the examiner which word you don't understand.
- The question word tells you what kind of information you should give. For example, if the examiner asks a question beginning with 'Why …', you should give a reason or reasons.
- Take care when you hear 'like' in a question: 'Do you like …?' has a completely different meaning to 'What is X like?'.
- Reply to the examiner's questions as fully as you can: don't just say 'Yes' or 'No'. You can make your reply full in various ways, such as giving examples.
- If you make a mistake while you are speaking, don't worry about it. You can correct yourself, or just continue speaking.
- Remember that the examiner will only assess your speaking ability, not the content of your replies: there are no 'right' or 'wrong' answers to the questions.

Useful language

Communication strategies

- *Pardon/Sorry?*
- *Could you say that again please?*
- *Would you mind repeating the question?*
- *What does X mean?*

Giving personal information

- *My name's X.*
- *People call me X.*
- *I come from X but I live in Y now.*

Talking about everyday life and habits

- *I usually/generally/sometimes/often …*
- *Every morning/day/week, I …*
- *On Mondays/Tuesdays …*
- *At the weekend, …*

In part two of the test, the examiner gives you a familiar topic to talk about. You are given a card with points to include in your talk, and you will have one minute to make notes before you begin.

Tips

- Read the card carefully, so that your talk is relevant to the topic you are given.
- Decide exactly what you will talk about (which person, place, occasion, etc.).
- Make a few notes about each separate point on the card (there are four things to include).
- Use the card and your notes as a plan.
- Begin talking when the examiner tells you to, and don't worry about the time: you will be told when to stop talking.
- Make sure you use the correct tense.
- When you are moving from one idea to another, make the change clear to the examiner by using linking words or phrases such as, 'Also …', 'Another thing I know is …'.
- If you make a mistake while you are speaking, don't worry about it. You can correct yourself, or just continue talking.

Useful language

Linking ideas and information

- *The place/person/occasion/activity I'm going to talk about is …*
- *First of all …*
- *Secondly …/Next …*
- *Another thing I should mention is …*
- *Regarding the X …*

Giving reasons

- *… because/so/so that …*
- *The main reason that …*

Expressing likes and dislikes

- *The thing I particularly like …*
- *I enjoyed it …*
- *It made me feel happy …*
- *I was really pleased …*
- *I didn't really like it …*

In Part 3 of the test the examiner will ask you some questions related to the topic of your talk in Part 2, and then discuss your replies with you. The questions will be more general and less personal than the questions in the other two parts.

Tips

- Listen very carefully to the question so that your reply is relevant.
- If you don't understand the question, ask the examiner to repeat it, or tell the examiner which word you don't understand.
- Reply to the examiner's questions as fully as you can. You can make your reply full in various ways, such as giving reasons for what you say, or providing examples.
- If you make a mistake while you are speaking, don't worry about it. You can correct yourself, or just continue speaking.
- Don't focus too much on accuracy while you are talking, as it might affect your fluency.
- Remember that the examiner will only assess your speaking ability, not the content of your replies: there are no 'right' or 'wrong' answers to the questions.

Useful language

Expressing an opinion

- *I'm not sure, but …*
- *I agree/don't really agree with that.*
- *I think people generally …*
- *I think one of the main reasons for this is …*
- *In my opinion it's better to …*
- *I'm not sure how important …*
- *Personally I'm against/in favour of …*

Comparing

- *X is better/bigger/easier/more common/less frequent than Y.*
- *Compared to X …*
- *More people… than …*
- *By contrast with X …*

Qualifying statements

- *To a certain extent …*
- *People tend to …*
- *In general …*
- *On the whole …*
- *It might/may/could be the case that …*
- *In certain circumstances …*
- *It's possible/likely/unlikely that …*

WRITING FILE

Test 1

ACADEMIC WRITING

WRITING TASK 1

Sample question

See Test 1, Task 1 on page 29.

Sample answer

The table shows the results of three surveys, conducted over 10 years, indicating changes in students' views about different aspects of provision at one undetermined university.

First of all, the most significant change is the considerable improvement in students' opinion of the electronic resources offered by this university. The number of positive responses almost doubled, increasing from 45 percent, in 2000, to 88 percent, in 2010. Another interesting point is a slight rise in the approbation of teaching quality. In 2000, the quality of teaching was commended by 65 percent of the students. By 2010, this figure had risen to 69 percent.

One aspect of university provision declined in popularity – ratings for the range of modules offered declined by 5 percent, from 32 percent in 2000 to 27 percent in 2010. Attitudes to print resources fluctuated slightly – positive responses rose from 87 percent in 2000 to 89 percent in 2005 but went down again to 88 percent in 2010. Finally, attitudes to buildings/teaching facilities were good and stable throughout at 77 percent.

The answer would get a high IELTS band because:

✓ A clear overview is presented at the beginning.
✓ There is a clear overall progression throughout the response.
✓ Key findings from the survey are clearly highlighted.
✓ Not every statistic is reported, indicating selection of data.
✓ There is some good use of cohesive devices ('First of all', 'Another interesting point', 'Finally').
✓ Some appropriately sophisticated vocabulary is used ('approbation of teaching quality').
✓ There are virtually no errors of grammar, spelling or punctuation.

Marking criteria

To gain the maximum number of marks, your answer to Task 1 should reach the required level according to the following criteria:

- **Task achievement** — It should be task-focused, free of irrelevant information and comment, and of the appropriate length.
- **Coherence and cohesion** — It should be organised in a logical sequence, with appropriate paragraph divisions, and should use linking words and phrases to show the reader what the connection between the different parts is.
- **Lexical resource** — The vocabulary should be accurate and appropriate.
- **Grammatical range and accuracy** — A variety of structures should be used as appropriate.

Exam help

- Look very carefully at the task input, including the instructions, the main title, the label on the two axes (graphs and bar charts), the column headings (tables), the segment labels (pie charts), the key, etc. Make sure that you understand the information you have been given before you begin writing.
- Decide what the main patterns are in the information. For example, what is the shape of the line in a line graph, and what does this show? Or, where there are two pie charts, how does the structure of one compare with the structure of the other?
- Make a brief plan. Decide how you will organise the information you are going to report. Start with the overall patterns and go on to support your statements with specific details from the visual.
- Write your answer according to your plan.
- Check the length of your answer.
- Read your answer through and make any changes which you think will improve it.
- Correct the grammar, spelling and punctuation as necessary.

Useful language

the proportion of X; the percentage of X; more than half of X; less than a third of X; a quarter

most of the X; some of the X; a bigger number of X … than of Y

rose; fell; increased sharply; gradually decreased; fluctuated; remained the same; went up;

went down; remained stable

over the whole period; during the first year; by the end of the period

shows that; indicates that; suggests that

Academic Writing Task 2

Sample question

See Test 1, Task 2 on page 29.

Sample answer

> It is a fact that, for a variety of reasons, people live longer than they used to. The question is: should this be a reason for raising the age at which people retire?
>
> One advantage of increasing the age at which people stop work is that it will help the state by generating more money. People in work pay the pensions of those in retirement, so the longer people stay in work, the less the rest of the population will have to pay towards pensions.
>
> Another advantage of having a later retirement age is that an occupation tends to keep people fulfilled and even healthier, and so it is beneficial to keep them working longer. Currently the normal retirement age is about 55 or 60. In the past, when people died younger, they could look forward to only a few years more life. Nowadays, they may have 30 or 40 years of leisure ahead of them, feeling that they no longer contribute anything valuable to society.
>
> However, for me the disadvantages of postponing retirement outweigh the advantages. Firstly, although older people obviously bring to their profession a great deal of experience, they gradually become less enthusiastic and less willing to adapt to changes. Young people are more adaptable and should not have to wait until their seniors leave to get a job. Secondly, many people simply don't want to spend so much of their lives working — they want to spend time with their children or grandchildren, or to use that time for things like travelling before they grow too old to enjoy it. I therefore feel the retirement age should be raised only slightly, if at all.

The answer would get a high IELTS band because:

✓ There is a clear, direct and original opening response to the task.

✓ The position is strong and consistent.

✓ Main points are clear and well-supported.

✓ Paragraphing is clear with central topics clearly signposted.

✓ Both sides of the debate are presented succinctly (although the task calls for the writer's opinion only, it is often helpful to explore the other side as well).

✗ The concluding line and point is a little minimal.

✓ Vocabulary – a good mix of straightforward language and sophisticated sentence construction.

✓ A wide range of structures is used.

✓ The majority of sentences are error-free.

✓ Punctuation is accurate throughout.

Marking criteria

These are more or less the same as for Task 1, except that the requirements for task achievement are rather more extensive.

Your answer should be task-focused and free of irrelevant information, and of the appropriate length, as for Task 1. At the same time, you will be expected to recognise the complexity of the essay topic, and where relevant, give an account of differing viewpoints and experiences. You should expand your ideas by providing explanations and examples, and most importantly, you should provide a clear conclusion for your essay, usually by stating your own position in relation to the topic.

As the content of the writing in Task 2 is longer and more complex than that for Task 1, it is even more important that you plan and organise your essay clearly, and create suitable paragraphs to reflect that organisation. In addition, connections between sentences and paragraphs should be made clear by the appropriate use of cohesive devices such as adverbials, relative pronouns and conjunctions.

Exam help

- Carefully read the statements and the question(s), which together represent the topic of your essay. Refer to these frequently as you plan your essay, to make sure that your writing is properly focused.
- Note down any ideas that come into your head.
- Make a plan. Select the ideas you want to use, and then decide how you will organise them.
- Write your answer according to your plan.
- Check the length of your answer.
- Read your answer through and make any changes which you think will improve it.
- Correct the grammar, spelling and punctuation as necessary.

Useful language

a lot of people; some people; many people; a few people

on the one hand … on the other hand; however; nevertheless; although

firstly; secondly; finally; then; next; furthermore; moreover; in addition; besides; as a result; for one thing … for another thing; by comparison

it appears that; it is apparent that; it seems that; this suggests that; people tend to; it is likely

that; in general; generally; usually; normally

in conclusion; to conclude; in summary

General Training

WRITING TASK 1

Sample question

See General Training Writing test, Task 1 on page 165.

Sample answer

Dear Simon,

How are you my friend? Are you enjoying your summer in Plymouth? I've heard that, unfortunately, the weather is very bad over there.

Well, as you're in England, I should ask you whether you could buy just a couple of things for me. You know that I'm a supporter of Plymouth Argyle Football Club, so could you just look round the city to find an official T-shirt of the current season, please? My size is M. I don't know if you can find them in Plymouth, but I also need the famous Scottish Chocolate Chip shortbread called 'Walkers'; I told you that both my parents adore them and so do I! Finally I also need a new wetsuit because the one I bought few years ago is too small now and I know that there are some good shops in Plymouth with that kind of things.

Could you buy this things for me and send them to me to my Italian address, please. Reply me as soon as possible, please, and enjoy your holiday.

The answer would get a high IELTS band because:

✓ Answers all the requirements of the task fully and clearly (although it might be better to focus on one, or possible, two items rather than three).

✓ The purpose of the letter is clear and the tone is very consistent and suitable for writing to a friend.

✓ The sequence of requests is logical and well separated.

✓ Opening is effective and appropriate to context.

✓ The vocabulary is sophisticated, natural and confidently used. There is good use of colloquial language suitable for an informal letter.

✓ There are very few grammatical errors.

✓ A wide range of sentence structures used and different tenses are used accurately.

✓ Good use of paragraphing.

Marking criteria

To gain the maximum number of marks, your answer to Task 1 should reach the required level according to the following criteria:

• **Task achievement and of the appropriate length.**	It should be task-focused, free of irrelevant information and comment.
• **Coherence and cohesion**	It should be organised in a logical sequence, with appropriate paragraph divisions, and should use linking words and phrases to show the reader what the connection between the different parts is.
• **Lexical resource**	The vocabulary should be accurate and appropriate.
• **Grammatical range and accuracy**	A variety of structures should be used as appropriate.

Exam help

- Look very carefully at the task input, that is: the description of the situation, the person you have to send a letter to, and the three points that you have to include. Decide whether the letter should be quite informal (e.g. if it is to a friend) or more formal (e.g. to an official).
- Decide what kind of information you will provide yourself, and make a few notes.
- Using the three bullet points as your plan, write your answer.
- Check the length of your answer.
- Read your answer through and make any changes which you think will improve it.
- Correct the grammar, spelling and punctuation as necessary.

Useful language

with reference to; concerning X; about X

unfortunately; I'm sorry to say that …; I'm afraid that …; fortunately; luckily

I'd be grateful if …; could you …; I'd like to …

Yours sincerely; Yours faithfully; Best wishes; Love

WRITING TASK 2

Sample question

See General Training Writing test, Task 2 on page 165.

Sample answer

The importance of cars is indisputable. Over the last few decades the significance of private transportation has steadily increased. In this essay, I'm going to discuss what factors favour more or fewer cars on the roads. The aspects I'm going to focus on are road design, safety and pollution.

First of all, I would like to consider whether there are too many cars or too small roads. Many towns and cities really seem spoilt by traffic but this may be mainly due to the narrowness of the streets. They really have to be widened so cars can get through easily, and lorries can transport goods more effectively on them.

Another reason for thinking that there are too many cars are the number of accidents caused by them. If we had fewer cars, fewer people would be injured or killed on our roads.

Damage to the environment is for many people the most important evidence that there is too much traffic on our roads. The effects on local areas are serious: Carbon monoxide and other harmful chemicals produced by cars damaging buildings and cause respiratory diseases and other health problems for residents. Noise and smells from cars also make our towns and cities less pleasant to live and work in. On a global scale, pollutants are changing our climate causing extreme weather which affects all our lives.

I believe strongly that we must reduce the number of cars in cities. Although most of us love our cars, and modern lifestyles make it difficult to stop our dependence on them, we should make fewer journeys and use public transportation more as an environment-friendly solution to traffic-clogged cities.

The answer would get a high IELTS band because:

✓ It covers all parts of the task.
✓ It presents a clear and consistent position throughout.
✓ The conclusion matches the position drawn throughout the response and is clearly and effectively presented.
✓ The ideas are supported by evidence.
✓ The ideas are logically organised and the answer progresses well.
✓ There is clear paragraphing and each paragraph has a clear central topic.
✓ There is a wide range of vocabulary ('indisputable', 'narrowness of the streets', 'on a global scale') which helps the writer present meaning precisely.

✓ There are hardly any errors in spelling and word formation.
✓ There is a wide range of complex structures is used.
✓ The punctuation is accurate throughout.

Marking criteria

These are more or less the same as for Task 1, except that the requirements for task achievement are rather more extensive.

Your answer should not contain irrelevant information or opinion, and it should be of the appropriate length. You should back up your ideas by providing explanations and examples, and most importantly, at the end of the essay you should provide a clear conclusion, usually by stating or re-stating your own viewpoint.

As the writing in Task 2 is longer and more complex than that for Task 1, it is even more important that you plan and organise your essay clearly, and create suitable paragraphs to separate the different ideas. You should also make the connections between sentences and paragraphs clear to your reader by using appropriate connectives such as *first*, *second*, *finally*, *however*, and *so*, as well as relative pronouns like *who* and *which*.

Exam help

- Carefully read the description of the problem or situation or opinion, and the question(s), which together represent the topic and purpose of your essay. Refer to these frequently as you plan your essay, to make sure that your writing is properly focused.
- Note down any ideas that come into your head.
- Select the ideas you want to use, and then decide how you will organise them.
- Write your answer according to your plan.
- Check the length of your answer.
- Read your answer through and make any changes which you think will improve it.
- Correct the grammar, spelling and punctuation as necessary.

Useful language

a lot of people; some people; many people; a few people

on the one hand … on the other hand; however; nevertheless; although

firstly; secondly; finally; then; next; furthermore; in addition; besides; as a result; for one thing … for another thing; by comparison

it appears that; it is apparent that; it seems that; this suggests that; people tend to; it is likely that; in general; generally; usually; normally

in conclusion; to conclude; in summary

ANSWER KEY

Please refer to the multi-Rom for the audioscripts.

Test 1

Test 1 LISTENING

SECTION 1

1 (an) accountant   **2** over 50
3 family (membership)   **4** nine/9   **5** doctor
6 (swimming) pool   **7** pay (extra)   **8** social events
9 air conditioning   **10** (the) restaurant

SECTION 2

11 E   **12** F   **13** B   **14** D   **15** C
16 G   **17/18** B/E   **19/20** A/D

SECTION 3

21 C   **22** A   **23** B   **24** A   **25** B
26 E   **27** G   **28** A   **29** D   **30** B

SECTION 4

31 ice age   **32** invisible   **33** infection(s)
34 flavour   **35** fungus/fungi   **36** sexes
37 extinction   **38** lowland   **39** shelter(s)
40 cuttings

Test 1 READING

READING PASSAGE 1

1	100/a hundred/ one hundred	PARAGRAPH 1 'For the island community of about a hundred residents… '
2	50 percent/ fifty percent	PARAGRAPH 1 '… CO_2 emissions … are 20 percent lower than the UK average, and electricity use is 50 percent lower.'
3	water	PARAGRAPH 2 '…most of its electricity from renewable sources, mainly water, wind and solar power.'
4	energy monitors	PARAGRAPH 3 'All households and businesses have energy monitors, which display current and cumulative electricity usage… '
5	diesel generators	PARAGRAPH 4 'Demand is also managed by warning the entire island when renewable energy generation is lower than demand, and diesel generators are operating to back it up… '
6	insulation	PARAGRAPH 6 'Eigg Heritage Trust has installed insulation in all of its own properties at no cost to the tenants…,'

7	greenhouses	PARAGRAPH 6 'The Trust also operates a Green Grants scheme, where residents can claim 50 percent of the cost of equipment … . Purchases included … greenhouses… '
8	F	PARAGRAPH 7 tells us that electricity *was* available prior to the installation of the grid, mostly via diesel generators.
9	T	PARAGRAPH 8 tells us that:*'The work by the Eigg Heritage Trust to reduce energy use has resulted in <u>significant reductions in carbon emissions</u> … '*
10	NG	The passage does say in PARAGRAPH 5 that: *'New energy supplies are being developed, including sustainably harvested forests to supply wood for heating'*, but this does not go as far as saying that wood will be the main source.
11	T	PARAGRAPH 9 tells us that: *'A reliable electricity supply has brought improvements …for example … the elimination of the constant noise of diesel generators.'*
12	F	PARAGRAPH 9 tells us that: *'Every household has the same five kW cap, irrespective of income …'*
13	T	PARAGRAPH 9 tells us of the variety of jobs created by the new electricity grid.

READING PASSAGE 2

14	F	PARAGRAPH F gives predictions of the numbers of temporary and home-based workers likely to be seen in 20 years time.
15	B	PARAGRAPH B explains that in the industrial age companies structured their organisations along mechanistic lines, i.e. *'systems of strict hierarchical structures and firm means of control.'*
16	G	PARAGRAPH G warns business leaders that the pace of change is fast and that they need to be aware of and to analyse factors which cause change in their world.
17	A	PARAGRAPH A describes the agricultural age which was one of *'relative organisational stability.'*

18	C	PARAGRAPH C shows that in the later part of the industrial age, demand for products was high, outstripping supply: this meant that customers were pleased to obtain goods and could not be too demanding about the particular features of the product.
19	D	PARAGRAPH D explains that: *'In the neo-industrial age …as technological advancements brought about increased productivity, supply overtook demand.'*
20	C	PARAGRAPH C notes that in the industrial age, organisations were: *'"task-oriented", with effort being put into increasing production through more effective and efficient production processes.'*
21	A	PARAGRAPH A describes the agricultural period as being one where both customer and labour markets were local.
22	D	PARAGRAPH D says that: *'In the neo-industrial age, people became more discriminating in the goods and services they wished to buy, … the emphasis moved towards adding value to goods and services …'*
23	B	PARAGRAPH B says that the industrial age *'was characterised by a series of inventions and innovations… '*
24	temporary	PARAGRAPH F *' … Leach anticipates that: "In 20 years time, 20-25 percent of the workforce will be <u>temporary</u> workers…"'*
25	home	PARAGRAPH F *' … 50 percent will work from <u>home</u> in some form.'*
26	factors	PARAGRAPH G *'… it is crucial that organisational managers and decision makers are aware of, and able to analyse the <u>factors</u> which trigger organisational change.'*

READING PASSAGE 3

27	A	PARAGRAPH 2 The author states that the fish were injected before and after the fish were trained: therefore A is the correct answer.

28	C	PARAGRAPH 4 *'Such findings suggest that our experiences create parallel, and possibly independent stages of memory, each with a different life span.'*
29	A	PARAGRAPH 5 The writer uses an example of an everyday task (walking up stairs) to illustrate how important to our lives it is to create immediate memory (A). B is tempting, but does not spell out the importance of memory creation to enable unconscious task performance. C is not dealt with in the fifth paragraph. D is not suggested.
30	D	PARAGRAPH 6 shows the observations by Kami and Sagi to confirm other findings: *'…there are also other kinds of evidence indicating more directly that the memories consolidate over time after learning …'* Kami and Sagi's work supported previous findings (D). It did not cast doubt on earlier work (as in A) and used a visual test (not involving hearing, as in C).
31	B	PARAGRAPH 7 *' … different regions of the brain were predominantly active at different times over a period of several hours after the training.'* (B) The experiment by Shadmehr and Holcomb used only one task, so A cannot be correct.' *They found that… subjects' performance remained stable for several hours after completion of the training.'* This contradicts C. There is no reference to a 'treatment', as in D.
32	NG	In PARAGRAPH 6 we learn that *'… the performance of human subjects trained in a visual skill did not improve until eight hours after the training was completed, and that improvement was even greater the following day.'* The passage does not say how often the training was given.
33	Y	PARAGRAPH 8 shows that the rats came to associate a tone of specific frequency with footshock.
34	Y	PARAGRAPH 8 *'… the selectivity of the neurons' response to the specific tone used in training continued to increase for several days after the training was terminated.'*

35	N	PARAGRAPH 9 contradicts the statement: *'It is not intuitively obvious why our lasting memories consolidate slowly.'*
36	NG	PARAGRAPH 9 *'All species of animals studied to date have both short- and long-term memory; and all are susceptible to retrograde amnesia.'* The passage does not show a difference between the stability of long term memory of humans and of other species, but neither does it specifically say they are the same.
37	F	PARAGRAPH 1 The answer must be 'new' as if subjects could already do the task they could not be 'trained' to do it.
38	E	PARAGRAPH 6 *'The hypothesis that lasting memory consolidates slowly over time is supported primarily by clinical and experimental evidence…'*
39	H	PARAGRAPH 9 *'…maybe we consolidate memories slowly because our mammalian brains are large and enormously complex. We can readily reject these ideas. All species of animals studied to date have both short- and long-term memory; and all are susceptible to retrograde amnesia.'*
40	A	PARAGRAPH 9 *'Consolidation of memory clearly emerged early in evolution, and was conserved.'*

Test 1 WRITING

Task 1 Model answer

The table shows the change in attitude, over ten years, of students at a particular university to different aspects of its academic provision.

Firstly, the most striking set of statistics relate to approval for electronic resources. There was a sharp increase in the number of students giving these resources a good rating, particularly in the first five years: from 45 percent in 2000, to 72 percent in 2005, and 88 percent in 2010. There was also an overall improvement in ratings for teaching quality, though the increase was relatively small (65 percent in 2000 rising to 69 percent in 2010) and there was a decline in the interim (63 percent in 2005). There was also a fluctuation in attitudes to print resources, rising from 87 percent to 89 percent in the first five years and then falling by one percent in 2010. Good ratings for the university's buildings and teaching facilities were identical throughout,

at 77 percent. Finally, there were poor ratings at the beginning of the period for the range of modules offered (32 percent in 2000) and they got worse, falling steadily from to 30 percent in 2005 and 27 percent in 2010.

Task 2 Model answer

Currently, in many countries, the age at which people stop paid work tends to be between 55 and 65. In the past, with few people living beyond the age of 80, it was rare for anybody to enjoy more than 20 years of retirement. However nowadays, that figure is much more likely to be 30, or even 40 years. This is often cited as a reason for requiring people to work to a later age.

Advocates of this point of view claim that it is extremely expensive to support people for so long in retirement. Pensions are paid for partly by people in their working lives, but today pension schemes usually yield far less money than necessary because they were designed to maintain people for much shorter periods. Increasingly, it is argued, the burden falls on younger people who end up working harder to pay for the enjoyment and relaxation of the old in their extended retirement. This, they say, is fundamentally unfair.

Although I acknowledge the validity of this argument, I believe it is outweighed by two very powerful counter-arguments. Firstly, when older people retire later they deprive young people of the opportunity to work and develop professionally. Secondly, I believe that people aren't just valuable members of society when they are earning money. Retired people can contribute a great deal through sharing in family responsibilities such as child care, and also in the wider community, by doing voluntary work. I think we should maintain the current retirement age and allow people to flourish in different ways when they finish paid employment.

Test 2

Test 2 LISTENING

SECTION 1
1 Lamerton   2 42 West Lane
3 11th June/11.06/06.11   4 cook   5 equipment
6 food-handling   7 First Aid   8 (college) tutor
9 0208 685114   10 colour/color blindness

SECTION 2
11 A	12 A	13 B	14 A	15 C
16 C	17 A	18 B	19 C	20 B

SECTION 3
21 C	22 G	23 A	24 E	25 F
26 D	27 G	28 C	29 A	30 E

SECTION 4
31 heavy   32 surgery   33 beetles   34 gas
35 moving   36 surface area   37 tubes
38 pressure   39 submarines/a submarine   40 fuel

READING PASSAGE 1

1	unfit	PARAGRAPH 2 '… many of the men who were assessed for military duty had been declared unfit.'
2	schools	PARAGRAPH 2 '… the solution in the providing of Physical Education (PE) programs in schools …,'
3	PE teachers	PARAGRAPH 2 '… better prepared and specifically educated PE teachers.'
4	surplus	PARAGRAPH 3 '… the surplus of Australians graduating with a PE degree … '
5	employment opportunities/ careers/routes	PARAGRAPH 3 '… obliged institutions delivering this qualification to identify new employment opportunities …'
6	T	PARAGRAPH 5 confirms that business people now see sport as having good potential as an investment.
7	NG	Although the passage shows that Rupert Murdoch has invested in a range of sport ventures, the passage does not state that he has a personal interest as distinct from a business interest.
8	T	PARAGRAPH 6 shows that there are:'new and developing career paths for graduates of human movement science, sport science, exercise science and related degrees.'
9	T	PARAGRAPH 7 shows the mutual dependence of business and university courses. Businesses need returns on their money, so universities must provide courses which enable this.
10	F	PARAGRAPH 8 notes the opposite, i.e. governments have focused too heavily on cure rather than prevention.
11	T	PARAGRAPH 8 says: 'If the change is not brought about for philosophical reasons, it will occur naturally, because insufficient funding will be available to address the ever-increasing costs of medical support.'
12	F	PARAGRAPH 9 says that graduates of human movement, exercise science and sport science degrees, 'who already have the skills, knowledge and understanding to initiate community health education programs …'
13	NG	There is nothing in the passage which comments on funding for sports science and related degrees.

READING PASSAGE 2

14	v	Paragraph A explains the size, output and costs of a large wind turbine for private use.
15	ii	Paragraph B estimates the greenhouse gas emissions (i.e. the environmental cost) involved in producing and installing the turbine.
16	iv	Paragraph C describes the carbon savings (i.e. the environmental benefits) of using a turbine to produce electricity rather than the typical grid.
17	ix	Paragraph D shows the financial incentives given by the UK government to encourage individuals to install turbines.
18	i	Paragraph E questions the government's spending on subsidies to individuals, arguing that the money may have been better spent on offshore wind farms.
19	vi	Paragraph F accepts that there has been some benefit in the subsidies to individuals.
20	viii	Paragraph G suggests that by spending on turbines individuals may have less money to spend on carbon-producing consumer goods.
21	B	PARAGRAPH A: '… a 15-kW micro-turbine … is capable of delivering 25,000 kilowatt-hours of electricity each year if placed on a suitable windy site.' PARAGRAPH D: 'The carbon investment pays back in just over a year, and every year after that is a 25-tonne carbon saving. (It's important to remember that all these sums rely on a wind turbine having a favourable location.)'(B)
22	E	PARAGRAPH D again: 'The UK government… introduced a subsidy for renewable energy that pays … producers … 24p per energy unit…'(E)
23	offshore wind farms	PARAGRAPH E '… had the government invested its money in offshore wind farms, instead of subsidising smaller domestic turbines, they would have broken even after eight years.'

24	developing technology	PARAGRAPH F 'In addition, such investment helps to promote and sustain <u>developing technology</u>.'
25	negative	PARAGRAPH G '... it is actually quite difficult to spend money without having a <u>negative</u> carbon impact.'
26	cars	PARAGRAPH G 'So if the subsidy encourages people to spend their money on a carbon-reducing technology such as a wind turbine, rather than on carbon-producing goods like <u>cars</u> ...'

READING PASSAGE 3

27	B	PARAGRAPH 2 'The pottery found includes a wide <u>variety of functional</u> types like storage jars, smaller containers, pouring vessels, cooking pots, drinking vessels and so on, which all relate to specific activities ...'
28	D	PARAGRAPH 2 'Given the <u>large number of shapes</u> produced ... it has generally been assumed that most ... Akrotiri pottery was produced by specialised craftsmen ...'
29	A	PARAGRAPH 4 'Standard measures may already have been in operation, such as those evidenced by a graduated <u>series of lead weights – made in disc form</u> – found at the site.'
30	E	PARAGRAPH 4 'The existence of units of capacity in Late Bronze Age times is also evidenced, by <u>the notation of units of a liquid measure for wine on excavated containers</u>.'
31	D	PARAGRAPH 5 '... <u>the length of a man's arm limits the size</u> of a smaller pot to a capacity of about twenty litres; that is also the maximum a man can comfortably carry.'
32	C	PARAGRAPH 8 '... it would be ... difficult for them to achieve the exact size required every time, without any mechanical means of regulating symmetry and wall thickness ... . Even where there is no noticeable external difference between pots meant to contain the same quantity of a commodity, differences in their capacity can actually reach one or two litres.'

33	NG	There is nothing in the passage to indicate whether there are plans for further excavation.
34	N	PARAGRAPH 3 '... there is <u>no real documentary evidence</u>. Our entire knowledge comes from the ceramic material itself ...'
35	Y	PARAGRAPH 5 '... the length of a man's arm limits the size of a smaller pot to a capacity of about twenty litres ...'
36	N	PARAGRAPH 6 '... merchants handling a commodity such as wine would have been <u>able to determine easily</u> the amount of wine they were transporting ...'
37	Y	PARAGRAPH 8 'In one case the deviation from the required size appears to be as much as <u>10 to 20</u> percent.'
38	Y	PARAGRAPH 9 '... regular trade routes within the Aegean led to increased movement of goods ... The increased demand for <u>standardised exchanges</u>, inextricably linked to commercial transactions, might have been one of the main factors which led to the standardization of pottery production.'
39	A	PARAGRAPH 8 'Even where there is no noticeable external difference between pots meant to contain the same quantity of a commodity, differences in their capacity can actually reach one or two litres.'
40	B	Only B summarises the overall purpose of the passage, showing the place of pottery production in Akrotiri within the overall socio-economic context.

Test 2 WRITING

Task 1 Model answer

The diagram shows the different stages in the process of converting an animal hide into leather goods.

The first stage is to hang out the hide on a line, in the open air to dry. After this, it is transported by lorry to the factory for processing. On arrival, it is submerged in vats of soap and water, and washed and then transferred to another vat where it is soaked in lime. Having been cleaned in this way, the hide is then sent to a large rolling machine where it is smoothed and flattened. In the next stage it is submerged in a liquid called tannin, which is a mixture of vegetable matter and water. This is followed by the polishing stage where small rollers are moved over the surface to produce a shine. The leather is then transported to a different factory where it is manufactured into the leather products we see in the shops, for example, shoes, handbags and sports equipment.

Task 2 Model answer

Although some people would argue that we don't change in any fundamental ways as we develop from young children to adults, I feel there are some marked differences in our social behaviour as we get older.

Firstly, most young children tend to express themselves much more openly than they do when older, showing great extremes of happiness and misery. However, when they are adults they learn to hide their real feelings. This can mean that children have very volatile relationships – for example, groups of youngsters will often fall out and row with each other at one moment, and then immediately afterwards they have mended their differences and are back as close companions. Some people say this change in behaviour is good, that showing extreme feelings is selfish and being a member of any community requires moderation of expression. Other people condemn this change, saying childish openness about feelings is more honest and as such, it should be valued. In many cultures there are proverbs which say something like 'truth comes from mouths of the very young', and adults sometimes lament the fact that they no longer feel things as deeply as they did when they were children. They regard this as a great loss.

In my view, it is a good thing if adults can retain some childlike qualities in their social behaviour throughout their life. I feel that, within reason, it is healthy to show feelings openly because it leads to stronger relationships. However, adults should always keep in mind the consequences of expressing what they feel the moment they feel it. They need to realise that sometimes saying what they feel is simply selfish and if it hurts others, then they should keep their thoughts to themselves.

Test 3

Test 3 LISTENING

SECTION 1
1	grey/gray	**2**	62,000	**3**	teacher
4	shopping	**5**	(£)1,100	**6**	tax
7	tyre/tire	**8**	headlight	**9**	Thursday
10	London				

SECTION 2
11	A	**12**	A	**13**	B	**14**	C	**15**	H
16	F	**17**	E	**18**	A	**19**	B	**20**	D

SECTION 3
21	C	**22**	C	**23**	A	**24**	B
25/26	B/E	**27/28**	C/D	**29/30**	B/D		

SECTION 4
31	English literature	**32**	autobiography
33	lab(oratory)	**34**	practical skills
35	novices/beginners	**36**	experimental
37	video	**38**	framework
39	editor		
40	sequence/order		

Test 3 READING

READING PASSAGE 1

1	10/ten million	PARAGRAPH 1 'At one time, there may have been as many as ten million of these little animals …'
2	cats and foxes/ foxes and cats	PARAGRAPH 1 '… their populations … were destroyed by the introduction of cats and foxes …'
3	monitored	PARAGRAPH 2 '… scientists from the Parks and Wildlife Commission of the Northern Territory monitored these two populations.'
4	fire	PARAGRAPH 2 '… a wild-fire destroyed the entire area occupied by the remaining colony.'
5	extinct	PARAGRAPH 2 '… in October 1991, a wild-fire destroyed the entire area occupied by the remaining colony. Thus the mala was finally pronounced extinct in the wild.'
6	5/five months	PARAGRAPH 3 '… the female can breed when she is just five months old …'
7	15/fifteen weeks	PARAGRAPH 3 '… the mother carries her young… in her pouch for about fifteen weeks …'
8	(strong) medicinal powers	PARAGRAPH 4 '… discuss this with the leaders of the Yapa people. Traditionally the mala had been an important animal in their culture, with strong medicinal powers for old people.'
9	skills and knowledge/ knowledge and skills	PARAGRAPH 4 'The skills and knowledge of the Yapa would play a significant and enduring role in this and all other mala projects.'
10	F	PARAGRAPH 5 shows that although an electric fence was able to protect the mala, they could not survive in the 'unfenced wild'.

11	T	PARAGRAPH 5 shows that the reintroduction programme had to be abandoned.
12	NG	There is no information in the passage as to whether the mala population size increased in size.
13	T	PARAGRAPH 7 confirms that the scientists felt the programme had surpassed their expectations.

READING PASSAGE 2

14	ii	Section A describes how in the seventeenth century Russian authorities used a variety of means to find out about and prevent the import of plague from foreign countries.
15	v	Section B shows that there was some success in preventing the import of the plague, though not total prevention.
16	i	Section C explains how Russian involvement in wars with other countries allowed the spread of the plague to Russian soldiers.
17	vii	Section D describes how the Tsar Peter 1 tried to limit the spread of the plague in a variety of ways.
18	iv	Section E summarises the measures taken by the Russian authorities as being limited in their success by being too piecemeal.
19	viii	Section F shows how a coherent preventive strategy was developed for more systematic control of plague.
20 and 21	B and D	PARAGRAPH A says that: 'Information on disease outbreak occurring abroad was regularly reported to the tsar's court through various means, including … undercover agents…'(B) PARAGRAPH B says that: '… foreign vessels were not allowed to dock in Russian ports if there was credible information about the existence of epidemics in countries from whence they had departed.'(D)
22 and 23	A and E	PARAGRAPH C explains that: '… none of the occurrences was of the same scale as in the past…'(A) PARAGRAPH E summarises the ad-hoc nature of the anti-plague measures: '… all of the measures had a provisional character: they were intended to respond to a specific outbreak, and were not designed as a coherent set of measures to be implemented systematically at the first sign of plague.'(E)

24	Astrakhan	PARAGRAPH F 'The first attempts to organise procedures and carry out proactive steps to control plague date to the aftermath of the 1727–1728 epidemic in Astrakhan.'
25	houses	PARAGRAPH F 'The houses of infected persons were to be burned along with all of the personal property they contained …'
26	fire	PARAGRAPH F '… letters brought by couriers were heated above a fire before being copied.'

READING PASSAGE 3

27	N	PARAGRAPH 1 states that: 'Even if the claims of misconduct and incompetence were eventually proven to be largely untrue, or confined to a few individuals, the damage was done. The perceived wrongdoings of a few people had raised doubts about the many.'
28	Y	PARAGRAPH 2 confirms the statement by saying that the scientists kept a low profile and hoped for the best.
29	N	PARAGRAPH 2 shows the reaction of news reports to be hostile.
30	Y	PARAGRAPH 3 says that: '[Ralph Cicerone] concluded that 'the perceived misbehavior of even a few scientists can diminish the credibility of science as a whole.'
31	NG	PARAGRAPH 4 Although the passage states that the US public's confidence in scientists, as a source of information about global warming, had dropped between 2008 and 2010, it does not tell us whether confidence has increased or decreased since 2010.
32	Y	In PARAGRAPH 6, the writer suggests that climate sciencsis should take professional advice to help to rebuild their reputation.
33	A	PARAGRAPH 7 The first step Gaines-Ross suggests 'take the heat – leader first', meaning that the heads should resign.
34	C	PARAGRAPH 9 says that, contrary to the PR advice, 'many climate researchers have avoided the media and the public …'

35	C	PARAGRAPH 12 says that climate scientists should not be '… *conceding to unfounded arguments which are based on prejudice rather than evidence …*'
36	D	PARAGRAPH 14 Uses the term marathon to indicate the time it will take to rebuild confidence: a marathon race being a long distance race rather than a short sprint.
37	C	PARAGRAPH 1 '… *some of the* <u>relevant statistics</u> *had been withheld from publication.*'
38	F	PARAGRAPH 6 '… *climate science needs professional help to rebuild its reputation. It could … follow the advice given by Leslie Gaines-Ross, a 'reputation strategist' at Public Relations (PR) company Weber Shandwick.*'
39	D	PARAGRAPH 6 '*In her recent book* '… <u>2 steps to safeguarding and recovering reputation</u>'. *Gaines-Ross's strategy …*'
40	A	PARAGRAPH 12 '*It is also important to engage with those* <u>critics</u>.'

Test 3 WRITING

Task 1 Model answer

Firstly, generally speaking, graduate unemployment rose for both groups from 2008 to 2009. Although women's unemployment levels were the same for April 2008, July 2008 and April 2009, all other figures rose. Secondly, there was generally more unemployment for both genders during the autumn and winter months, with figures for both genders peaking in October (e.g. for males: 16 percent in October 2008 and 22 percent October 2009).

Perhaps the most striking trend, though, is for a greater percentage of male than female graduates to be out of work at all times of the year. Also there is greater seasonal variation for men than women: the gender difference is much more marked in October of both years and this reaches a peak in October 2009, where there is an eight percent difference between women and men.

Finally, employment of women graduates is relatively stable throughout the whole two-year period. It only varies by eight percent (six percent in April 2008, to 14 percent in October 2009). By contrast, men's unemployment fluctuates more noticeably, with a range from eight to 22 percent.

Task 2 Model answer

Many people make the assumption that the production of more and more goods is always a good thing for all economies. They say that this growth generates wealth, not just for the wealthy few but for all strata of society. They argue that increasing production brings immediate benefit to rich industrialists but that, in turn, they provide employment for, and buy goods and services from, other less wealthy people in the community. Also it is argued that the wealthy individuals will pay more in taxes and thus the money from growth will benefit everyone, through improved health and education, and that a happier, more stable and more developed society will result.

However, other people argue that such growth in production can have the opposite effect. They contend that any riches tend to be claimed by the few and trickle down to very few others in the community. Also, wealthy people know how to use a variety of devious measures to evade paying tax. Another argument against such growth is that even if this wealth <u>does</u> filter down to all citizens it does not, in itself, bring about a better society. Instead it can produce a consumerist mentality which draws a simple equation between having 'things' and being happy. This is bad for the moral and spiritual life of the country and also can damage the environment as people want more and more objects, creating pollution through production and disposal of waste.

On balance, I feel that a compromise position is the healthiest one – some economic growth should be encouraged as long as there are safeguards intended to ensure fair distribution of wealth and reduce the negative impact on the environment.

Test 4

Test 4 LISTENING

SECTION 1
1 hairdresser 2 tablets 3 sunglasses
4 lock 5 adaptor/adapter 6 taxi
7 Jefferey 8 0777594128 9 church
10 30th April/30.04/04.30

SECTION 2
11 C 12 A 13 A 14 C 15 B
16 C 17/18 D/E 19/20 C/E

SECTION 3
21 C 22 B 23 C 24 A 25/26 C/E
27/28 D/E 29/30 C/E

SECTION 4
31 call centre 32 inconclusive
33 methodology/methods 34 unequal
35 female/women 36 response 37 control
38 sample/group 39 their/other colleagues
40 confidential

READING PASSAGE 1

1	T	PARAGRAPH 2 'His father … ran the Brash retail music business that had been founded in 1862 … <u>specialising in pianos</u>.'
2	F	PARAGRAPH 3 Brash's first job was with Myer department stores before he joined the family business.
3	T	PARAGRAPH 3 'After initially complaining of his <u>extravagance</u>, his father grew to accept the change, and gave Geoff increasing responsibility …'
4	T	PARAGRAPH 4 tells us that after World War II Brash's had focussed on 'white goods' before Geoff Brash took over in 1957.
5	NG	Although the passage describes relationships with businesses in Japan and China, it does not tell the reader if Brash considered opening stores in other countries.
6	(a) share scheme	PARAGRAPH 5 'Alfred Brash had also been a pioneer in introducing a share scheme for his staff …'
7	Roland/ Roland group/ the Roland group	PARAGRAPH 6 'He developed a relationship with …, the founder of Japan's <u>Roland group</u> …'
8	(a) trade fair	PARAGRAPH 7 'In 1965, Brash … attended a <u>trade fair</u>…'
9	jazz	PARAGRAPH 7 '… a trip that reintroduced <u>jazz</u> to many Chinese musicians.'
10	1998	PARAGRAPH 8 'The company was sold to Singaporean interests and continued to trade until <u>1998</u> …'
11	education	PARAGRAPH 9 '… promoting multi-media music making and education for teachers and students.'
12	technology	PARAGRAPH 9 '… offer teachers and young people the opportunity to get exposure to the latest music technology …'
13	branches	PARAGRAPH 9 'The organisation has now also established branches in New Zealand, South Africa and Ireland, as well as … Australia.'

READING PASSAGE 2

14	iii	PARAGRAPH A identifies the variety of occupations undertaken around the Thames river in medieval times and outlines what each involved.
15	vi	PARAGRAPH B describes the physical difficulties of transporting goods and the ways men worked to overcome those.
16	ix	PARAGRAPH C outlines the change in status of river work over the centuries, from well-regarded in the fourteenth – eighteenth centuries to disreputable in the late eighteenth and early nineteenth centuries.
17	iv	PARAGRAPH D describes the composition of 'a workforce of many thousands congregated in a relatively small area.'
18	ii	PARAGRAPH E shows the river community as being '… a world apart with its own language and laws.'
19	vii	PARAGRAPH F outlines the great numbers of people employed on a casual basis compared to a relatively small number of permanent workers.
20 and 21	C and E	Paragraph A identifies nine different occupations of workers making their living by the river.(C) Paragraph B details the heavy lifting and carrying required of the men when quays and streets were unsuitable for wagons or large carts.(E)
22 23	A and C	Paragraph D notes the many thousands of people employed in a small area and describes the East End as 'the most intensively inhabited region of London.'(A) Paragraph F notes '… crowds of casuals waiting for work at the dock gates …' and '… some 2,500 casual workers who were hired by the shift.'(C)
24	regular wage	PARAGRAPH F '… 400–500 permanent workers who earned a <u>regular wage</u> … But there were some 2,500 casual workers who were hired by the shift.'

25	steam power	PARAGRAPH F '<u>Steam power</u> could not be used for the cranes … because of the danger of fire.'
26	picturesque	PARAGRAPH F 'This was part of the life of the river unknown to those who were intent upon its more <u>picturesque</u> aspects.'

READING PASSAGE 3

27	NG	Although the passage tells us in PARAGRAPH 1 how many preschool children in the US had played video games, there is no comparison with usage in other countries.
28	Y	PARAGRAPH 1 says: '… we predict that preschoolers will both continue and increasingly begin to adopt video games for personal enjoyment.'
29	NG	Although we are told in PARAGRAPH 1 that 'once a game system enters the household it is potentially available for all family members, including the youngest' this does not necessarily mean that parents are explicitly giving their permission for children to use the game.
30	N	PARAGRAPH 2 notes that research in this field tends to focus on marketing and fault finding rather than original design for targeted users.
31	Y	PARAGRAPH 2 says that '… research has to be undertaken in order to truly understand those audiences, [preschoolers or senior citizens] their abilities, their perspective, and their needs.'
32	C	PARAGRAPH 4 'In addition to their still developing motor skills … many of the major stumbling blocks are cognitive.'
33	E	PARAGRAPH 5 'they are less exact with their stylus movements … [but] their fingers are so small that they mimic the stylus very effectively, and therefore by using their fingers they can often be more accurate in their game interactions.'
34	F	PARAGRAPH 4 'Though preschoolers … understand that pictures can stand for real-life objects …'

35	A	PARAGRAPH 4 '… preschoolers may be unable to understand that there is a direct link between how the controller is used and the activities that appear before them on screen.'
36	I	PARAGRAPH 4 '… the vast majority are still unable to read and write. Thus, using text-based menu selections is not viable.'
37	B	PARAGRAPH 3 tells us that in 2007 staff at Nickelodeon had an idea that their new Nintendo DS might be suitable for preschoolers.
38	C	PARAGRAPH 3 shows that the aim of the study was to find out what preschoolers might be able to do with a hand-held game and what the literature could tell them about child development.
39	A	PARAGRAPH 5 suggests that one of the limitations of game cartridges is the limited memory capacity and that spoken instructions use a lot of memory.
40	B	B is the best title as the passage deals with a piece of research which helped to design video games for preschool children. The passage does not deal with the issues.'

Test 4 WRITING

Task 1 Model answer

The two pie charts show that low and high income groups spend their disposable income (earnings excluding house rent or purchase) on similar items but in different proportions.

Regarding the low income group, the highest proportion of their money is spent on food and drink – 29 percent, compared to just 15 percent for the high income group. This is closely followed by 24 percent paid out on fuel bills, which contrasts with a much lower figure for this item for the high income group (only 7 percent). The most popular item for the high earners is recreation and cultural activities – 21 percent compared with 11 percent by the low earning group. The higher group also spend a much higher proportion than the lower income group on restaurants and hotels (12 percent and 4 percent respectively) and on transportation (16 percent and 9 percent respectively). The proportion of expenditure on clothing for the two groups is very similar, with only one percent difference between the two (six percent for high income group and five percent for the low).

Task 2 Model answer

Few would argue that technologies developed in recent years have had a significant impact on the way books and music are shared. The Internet enables very cheap, or even completely free, access to words and sounds.

For many people this is a very negative development. Firstly, they make the point that downloading words and music without paying is morally wrong – it is, after all, a form of stealing, just as much as if someone had shop-lifted a CD. Secondly, they claim that if nobody actually buys music or books then the people who produce them, for example, novelists, journalists or musicians, will no longer be able to make a living from such work. Eventually new work will stop being created, no one will perform live and whole industries will cease to function. They say that eventually the only way to make money from writing and music will be through things like celebrity endorsements, and mediocrity will flourish.

I believe, however, that freer access to books and music on the Internet is a liberating development, allowing more people to enjoy what was once the preserve of the few. It is particularly good that young people can freely experience a wide range of music and writing. I feel the only way to prevent accessing books and music is by stricter monitoring and harsher penalties and that this would be extremely damaging, because it would increase surveillance and control. I believe it would stifle creativity and undermine creative industries much more than free access is said to do now. I believe writers and musicians will find a way of benefiting from the new situation and good artists will be able to make a living as they always have done.

Test 5

Test 5 LISTENING

SECTION 1
1   weekend(s)   2   plasdeco   3   clear
4   late/unreliable   5   cheaper   6   messy
7   designs   8   expensive   9   painting
10   ladder(s)

SECTION 2
11   B   12   C   13   A   14   B   15   C
16   C   17   I   18   H   19   D   20   G

SECTION 3
21   D   22   B   23   A   24   H   25   F
26   E   27/28   B/E   29/30   A/C

SECTION 4
31   common   32   woodland/woods/forest(s)   33   tail
34   grey/gray   35   humans/people   36   memory
37   hearing   38   birds   39   year   40   water

Test 5 READING

READING PASSAGE 1

1	F	PARAGRAPH 2 tells that *'… in a coral-reef fishery the physical accessibility of the reef opens up opportunities for direct participation by women …'*

2	T	PARAGRAPH 2 goes on to say that by being able to directly participate in coral-reef fishing, the independence and importance of women are enhanced.
3	T	PARAGRAPH 2 shows that the coral-reef enables *to acquire important skills and knowledge for later life.*
4	T	PARAGRAPH 3 confirms that on Ulithi Atoll *'women have a distinct role, and rights, in the distribution of fish catches.'*
5	NG	While the passage notes in PARAGRAPH 3 that the canoes are *'made from mahogany logs from nearby Yap Island … '*, it does not specify where the canoes are actually constructed.
6	F	PARAGRAPH 3 tells us that reef fisheries give women greater control over the household income and allow them to in negotiate for loans or credit.
7	F	PARAGRAPH 4 says that coral reef fisheries are *'relatively stable compared with other fisheries, or land-based agricultural production.'*
8	sea cucumbers	PARAGRAPH 5 *'In Palau, sea cucumbers growing on the reef are seldom eaten during good weather in an effort to conserve their populations.'*
9	agricultural	PARAGRAPH 6 *'… in coastal communities in northern Mozambique, reef harvests provide key sources of food and cash when agricultural production is low …'*
10	scuba diving	PARAGRAPH 7 *'In the Caribbean alone, tours based on scuba-diving …'*
11	communi-cations	PARAGRAPH 7 *'The upgrading of roads and communications … may also bring benefits to local communities.'*
12	sustain-ability	PARAGRAPH 7 *'There is growing recognition that sustainability is a key requirement …'*
13	conflict	PARAGRAPH 8 *'Where tourism development has not been carefully planned … conflict has sometimes arisen between tourism and local, small-scale fishers.'*

READING PASSAGE 2

14	v	The theme of PARAGRAPH A is that *'… in order to learn science, people often have to change the way they think in ordinary situations …'*

15	ii	PARAGRAPH B illustrates the problem of superficial understanding by explaining how students can learn information but be unable to apply it.
16	vi	PARAGRAPH C explains Piaget's idea that learning results from conflicts between existing concepts and new information which challenges them.
17	i	PARAGRAPH D shows that 'discovery learning' had initially been seen as a lone learner being challenged to re-think, but later the role peers can play in learning had been proposed.
18	ix	PARAGRAPH E outlines a study in which it was found that *'progress was … observed … in a second test given around four weeks after the group work.'*
19	viii	PARAGRAPH F describes a study which investigated whether the exchange of ideas in pair work could aid learning.
20 and **21**	B and D	PARAGRAPH C According to Piaget, learning takes place when pupils are actively engaged in solving problems that challenge their current thinking (B). Although the teacher is important (as in A), it is the inner dynamics of the pupil's thinking which is key. Young children – according to Piaget – do not always accept the need to change their ideas in the face of new and conflicting information: they may reject the new information to preserve their old way of thinking.(D) Repetition and consistency of input (C) is not mentioned and children's ability to help each other (E) was not noted by Piaget.
22 and **23**	A and E	PARAGRAPH E *'Howe compared the progress of 8–12 year-old children in understanding what influences motion down a slope.'* (A)
		Howe and colleagues created two groups according to *a pre-test; a post test was given immediately after the sessions and another four weeks later.* (E) The children did not work in mixed-ability groups (B); the talkativeness of the children is not mentioned (C); the teacher was not actively involved (D).

24	discovery learning	PARAGRAPH D *'Piaget's hypothesis about how cognitive change occurs was later translated into an educational approach which is now termed "discovery learning".'*
25	teacher	PARAGRAPH D *'Discovery learning initially took what is now considered the 'lone learner' route. The role of the* <u>teacher</u> *was to select situations that challenged the pupils' reasoning …'*
26	peers/ friends	PARAGRAPH D *'… it was subsequently proposed that interpersonal conflict, especially with* <u>peers</u>*, might play an important role in promoting cognitive change.'*

READING PASSAGE 3

27	D	PARAGRAPH 2 emphasises the fascination monumental ruins hold for us and our wonder at the mysteries they hold. This might be termed a 'romantic' appeal.
28	C	PARAGRAPH 3 *'This suspicion of unintended ecological suicide (ecocide) has been confirmed … by archaeologists, climatologists, historians, paleontologists, and palynologists (pollen scientists).'*
29	A	PARAGRAPH 4 notes that many civilisations *'declined rapidly after reaching peak numbers and power …'*
30	Y	PARAGRAPH 5 *'Today many people feel that environmental problems overshadow all the other threats to global civilisation.'*
31	Y	PARAGRAPH 5 notes the build up of toxic substances as one of four new environmental threats.
32	N	PARAGRAPH 5 shows that there is much debate about the seriousness of the current environmental problems.
33	NG	The passage states in PARAGRAPH 6 that: *'We differ from past societies in some respects that put us at lower risk than them … We also differ from past societies in some respects that put us at greater risk than them'* but it does not compare individual societies past and present.

34	Y	The final sentence of PARAGRAPH 6 warns us that we can learn lessons from the past but we must be careful about the comparisons.
35	C	PARAGRAPH 2 'The monumental ruins left behind by those past societies hold a fascination for all of us.'
36	A	PARAGRAPH 4 '… it [is] tempting to draw analogies between the course of human societies and the course of individual human lives… But that metaphor proves erroneous for many past societies …'
37	F	PARAGRAPH 5 'These environmental problems include the same eight that undermined past societies, plus four new ones …'
38	D	PARAGRAPH 6 '… some of those [differences] often mentioned include our powerful technology (i.e. its beneficial effects) … We also differ from past societies in some respects that put us at greater risk than them: again, our potent technology (i.e. its unintended destructive effects) …'
39	E	PARAGRAPH 6 'We shouldn't be so naïve as to think that study of the past will yield simple solutions, directly transferable to our societies today.'
40	A	Only A sums up the argument. The issues mentioned in B, C and D are either not referred to in the passage or form only a small part of the argument.

Task 1 Model answer

The graph shows the average weather conditions in one region of East Africa. It shows that there are significant differences in the average monthly precipitation and some variation in temperature. The range of rainfall figures is very large across the year (from approximately five to 280 millimetres) whereas the temperature only fluctuates by three degrees, from 20.5–23.5°C.

Broadly speaking, in this region periods of high rainfall tend also to be periods of slightly hotter weather, with two noticeable peaks in the year. Temperatures are fairly high in March and April (just over 23°C), which coincides with a time of very heavy rainfall (with a top figure of 280mm in April). Both rainfall and temperature figures fall in the middle of the year (to a yearly low of 20.5°C, and just five mm of rain in July).

The exception to this pattern – of warmer weather being damper – is January/February and September where there are relatively high temperatures (22–23°C) but low rainfall (less than 20mm).

Task 2 Model answer

I strongly agree with the suggestion that humankind should consume less meat and instead have more vegetables in their diet, and I believe that a number of steps can be taken to persuade people to do this.

Firstly, I feel that education has a major role to play in bringing about this change of lifestyle. A well-informed minority of the world's population may be fully aware of the fact that it is much cheaper and more environmentally sound to eat vegetables, thereby cutting out one whole stage of production, rather than consuming the animals which graze on vegetation. However, I believe that the majority are not conscious of this. Figures should be made widely available showing the savings to be made from this option – both financial and ecological. From a young age, children should also be taught this as an essential part of the curriculum and to set an example, school meals should be redesigned to reflect a shift from meat to vegetables.

A second measure would be financial. Taxes can be put on meat to make it a luxury item to be eaten fairly rarely, at most three of four times a week, rather than two or three times a day as is the practice in many parts of the developed world. There is, however, a danger in too much interference in people's choice. It is often the case that resistance builds up against lecturing and fiscal penalties, meaning that people will react by ignoring all the advice. Perhaps a compromise position would be to encourage less wastage in food production and retail, particularly in the developed world. Huge amounts of perfectly usable food are thrown away by households and restaurants and supermarkets. Less wastage would mean less food production in the first place.

Test 6

SECTION 1

1 Moonfleet   2 fields   3 shops
4 summerhouses   5 river   6 dining
7 sea   8 garden   9 parking   10 agent

SECTION 2

11 A   12 B   13 C   14 B
15/16 B/D   17/18 A/C   19/20 B/E

SECTION 3

21 A   22 B   23 A   24 C   25 B
26 B   27 B   28 A   29 D   30 C

SECTION 4

31 (very) thin   32 court documents
33 high-quality   34 buried   35 thickness
36 bleached/whitened   37 dialect   38 baseline
39 evolution   40 trade routes

READING PASSAGE 1

1	labels	PARAGRAPH 1 'During the 1950s ...There were no celebrity designers or models, nor were there any labels ...'
2	bargain	PARAGRAPH 1 'even ... high-society women... were proud of getting a bargain'
3	plastic	PARAGRAPH 2 '[In] the 1960s...[there was] an acceptance of innovative types of material such as plastic and coated polyester.'
4	traditional	PARAGRAPH 3 'The following decade witnessed an increase in the export of traditional materials ...'
5	masculine	PARAGRAPH 4 'In India too, contours became more masculine ...'
6	showy	PARAGRAPH 5 'designers decided to get themselves noticed by making showy outfits ...'
7	ethnic	PARAGRAPH 6 'In the last decade of the millennium, the market shrunk and ethnic wear made a comeback.'
8	T	PARAGRAPH 7 tells us that at the beginning of the 21st century, new designers and models, and more sensible designs helped the Indian fashion industry accelerate once again.
9	NG	Although the passage tells us in PARAGRAPH 7 that '... India is the third largest producer of cotton ...' it does not tell us how much cotton India exports.
10	T	PARAGRAPH 8 describes the many advantages enjoyed by the Indian garment and fabric industries.
11	F	PARAGRAPH 8 makes it clear that changes in the rate of exchange between the rupee and the dollar have depressed prices, making exports more attractive.
12	F	PARAGRAPH 9 tells us that in Chapa the range and quality of raw silks churned out here are good despite the crude production methods and equipment.
13	T	PARAGRAPH 9 describes the popularity of fabric designs originally used for a simple wrap, and use of beads for accessory items and evening wear.

READING PASSAGE 2

14	H	PARAGRAPH H 'This report, therefore, is structured around the individual components of a sustainable community, ...'
15	D	PARAGRAPH D '... the town is bisected by the east–west railway, and people living in Ladygrove ... felt and still feel cut off from the town and its community.'
16	G	PARAGRAPH G '... from now on public finance will need to provide a greater proportion of infrastructure project costs.'
17	C	PARAGRAPH C '... the development of job opportunities in the railway industry, and in a large, military ordnance depot was the spur to Didcot's expansion.'
18	I	PARAGRAPH I '... discussions with the local community about their aspirations for the town as well as other stakeholders, will be undertaken ...'
19	E	PARAGRAPH E 'In 1990 public-sector finance was used to buy the land required for the Orchard Centre development, comprising a superstore, parking and a new street of stores running parallel to Broadway.'
20	C	PARAGRAPH C 'Didcot failed to develop Broadway as a compact town centre, and achieved only a strip of shops along one side of the main street hemmed in by low density housing and service trade uses.'
21	E	PARAGRAPH E 'Population growth in the new housing areas failed to spark adequate private-sector investment... and the limited investment which did take place – Didcot Market Place development ...'
22	A	PARAGRAPH E '... the Orchard Centre development, comprising a superstore, parking and a new street of stores ...'

23	D	PARAGRAPH F '… the improved railway crossing at Marsh Bridge … Such projects were delayed due to <u>difficulties in securing public finance</u>.'
24	low cost/affordable	PARAGRAPH G '… the requirement for developers that forty percent of the units in a new housing development should be <u>low cost homes</u> …'
25	infrastruc-ture	PARAGRAPH H 'The Government's Sustainable Communities Plan seeks a holistic approach to new urban development in which … <u>infrastructure</u> of all kinds are carefully planned and delivered …'
26	strategic master plan	PARAGRAPH I 'discussions with the local community … as well as other stakeholders, will be undertaken … and will lead to the development of a <u>strategic master plan</u>.'

READING PASSAGE 3

27	Y	PARAGRAPH 1 says that one of the most influential ideas is that of universal grammar which prevailed from the 1960s for the next five decades.
28	N	PARAGRAPH 2 shows that 'linguists have identified many universal language rules. However, there are almost always exceptions.'
29	Y	PARAGRAPH 3 confirms that some linguists are controversial in arguing that languages, such as Straits Salish do not even have distinct nouns or verbs.
30	NG	Although the passage tells us that some linguists are pleased to move away from the search for universal language rules, it does not say if this is a majority of linguists.
31	N	PARAGRAPH 5 The Evans and Levinson ideas suggest that human brains are different depending on the language environment.
32	Y	PARAGRAPH 5 '… every time a language becomes extinct, humanity loses an important piece of diversity.'

33	A	PARAGRAPH 6 '… any given language is a complex system shaped by many factors, including culture, genetics and history.'
34	C	PARAGRAPH 7 Linguistic elements may build on human reasoning. We perceive the world in a certain way before we learn to speak.
35	C	PARAGRAPH 8 Notes that middle ear infections are common among indigenous Australian children and their language lacks sounds which would be difficult to hear, given an ear infection. There may be a cause-and-effect relationship here.
36	B	PARAGRAPH 9 'Levinson and Evans are not the first to question the theory of universal grammar, but no one has summarised these ideas quite as persuasively'.
37	D	The passage compares in an objective manner the differing views of linguists.
38	B	PARAGRAPH 2 '… Arrernte … has VC syllables but no CV syllables.'
39	A	PARAGRAPH 3 'Others, such as Lao … have no adjectives at all.'
40	D	PARAGRAPH 4 'Even apparently indisputable universals have been found lacking. This includes recursion … Amazonian Piraha does not have this quality.'

Test 6 WRITING

Task 1 Model answer

The plans show the changes to a health centre over the last six years. Since 2005, the centre has expanded in a number of different ways. Firstly, an extension has been added to accommodate a minor operations room. Also, the interior has been significantly remodelled. In 2005, there was a large entrance area with wide doors and a lot of open space for waiting, with the reception desk in the middle. There were only three consulting rooms and a physiotherapy room. This room has stayed the same size but the consulting rooms have been made smaller and increased to four in number. The office has been made smaller and the reception desk put in front of it. A children's play area has been added in the corner near the entrance.

Outside there have also been changes. The car park has been expanded with room for 18 more cars. The garden is decreased in size to accommodate the extra parking space.

Task 2 Model answer

In many parts of the world, and in many different sectors, more and more people are staying at home rather than commuting to work.

Opponents of home-working say that being together in a workplace with colleagues is an important part of keeping people healthy and happy. Staying at home, never meeting people can lead to depression. They also say that, from a professional point of view, it is important to spend time in formal and less formal situations with co-workers. Although it is argued that interaction can happen via computers, especially with a visual element such as video conferencing, they don't believe this can ever replace face to face contact.

For me, the advantages of working from home more than outweigh the disadvantages. Firstly, many workers prefer home working, saying they function more effectively because they can relax, without the pressure and waste of the long commute. With new technologies placing people in the same room metaphorically, it is becoming much easier to do this. With less travel there is a smaller carbon footprint, although this is a claim which has yet to be proved because many people choose to live in remoter areas and car use is not significantly reduced when working at home.

Finally, what clinches the argument for me is the fact that working at home enables many people to join the workforce who would not otherwise be able to do so. This option is particularly liberating for women because they often have more caring responsibilities.

To sum up, I believe strongly that working from home is the fairest and most efficient option for most people.

Test 7

Test 7 LISTENING

SECTION 1

1   terminal   2   Pantera   3   east
4   07765 328411   5   hotel (restaurant)   6   raincoat
7   (walking) shoes   8   Mountain Lives
9   chocolate(s)   10   (a) calendar

SECTION 2

| 11 C | 12 B | 13 A | 14 A | 15 C |
| 16 B | 17 F | 18 B | 19 D | 20 E |

SECTION 3

21/22 A/D   23/24 B/E   25/26 B/C
27 C   28 B   29 D   30 F

SECTION 4

31 rainfall   32 air/plane   33 freezing
34 unsuccessful   35 cheap/inexpensive

36 grass   37 solar   38 site/location/place
39 walls   40 women

Test 7 READING

READING PASSAGE 1

1	hot tar	PARAGRAPH 3 '... hot tar onto which a layer of stone chips was laid – became known as "tarmacadam" ...'
2	5/five cm/centimetres	PARAGRAPH 3 'Immediately above this ... and ... compacted to a thickness of just five centimetres ...'
3	water	PARAGRAPH 3 '...stone dust mixed with water ...'
4	F	PARAGRAPH 2 says that new roads were generally of inferior quality, and that the achievements of Roman builders were largely unsurpassed until the eighteenth century.'
5	NG	Although PARAGRAPH 4 states that privately owned toll roads were built in the nineteenth century, it does not comment on who could afford to use them.
6	T	PARAGRAPH 5 confirms that the advent of heavy traffic meant that roads were inadequate: '... the ever-increasing use of motor vehicles threatened to break up roads built to nineteenth-century standards ...'
7	NG	Paragraph 7 details the development of high speed roads but does not mention the use or non-use of speed restrictions.
8	Romans	PARAGRAPH 8 'The development by the Romans of the arched bridge ...'
9	stone	PARAGRAPH 8 'Most were built of stone ...'
10	light	PARAGRAPH 10 'Such bridges are nevertheless light ...'
11	longest	PARAGRAPH 10 'The 1998 Akashi Kaikyo Bridge in Japan has a span of 1,991 metres, which is the longest to date.'
12	steel	PARAGRAPH 11 'Cantilever bridges ... exploit the potential of steel construction ...'
13	stable	PARAGRAPH 11 'Although the suspension bridge can span a wider gap, the cantilever is relatively stable ...'

READING PASSAGE 2

14	C	PARAGRAPH B *Homo neanderthalensis* lived in Europe and parts of Asia, as did *Homo sapiens*.
15	B	PARAGRAPH B '... interlopers in the form of *Homo sapiens*, who were spreading out from Africa.'
16	A	PARAGRAPH B '... the arrival of *Homo sapiens* in a region was always quickly followed by the disappearance of Neanderthals.'
17	C	PARAGRAPH E tells us that the two species, i.e. *Homo neanderthalensis* and *Homo sapiens* were inter-fertile.
18	A	PARAGRAPH E says that '... no Neanderthal mitochondrial DNA has turned up in modern humans.'
19	D	PARAGRAPH D explains the change in thinking about the relationship between the two species: 'Previous genetic analysis ... had suggested no interbreeding between Neanderthals and modern humans. The new ... examination ... shows this conclusion is wrong.'
20	B	The final sentence of PARAGRAPH B explains that we do not yet know why the arrival of *Homo sapiens* in a region was always quickly followed by the disappearance of Neanderthals.
21	G	PARAGRAPH G says that Neanderthals and modern humans share the same version of a gene which is involved in the ability to speak.
22	A	PARAGRAPH A sets out the groundbreaking nature of the analysis by Svante Paabo and his colleagues.
23	E	PARAGRAPH E notes that it is strange, 'that no Neanderthal mitochondrial DNA has turned up in modern humans, since the usual pattern of invasion in historical times was for the invaders' males to mate with the invadeds' females.'
24	inter-breeding /crossbreed-ing	PARAGRAPH E '... even after several hundred thousand years of separation, the two species were <u>inter-fertile</u>.'

25	shape/ growth	PARAGRAPH G 'The newly evolved regions of DNA also include a gene called RUNX2, which controls bone growth. That may account for differences in the <u>shape</u> of the skull ...'
26	little-finger bone	PARAGRAPH G 'Another of his teams has revealed the existence of a hitherto unsuspected species of human, using mitochondrial DNA found in a <u>little-finger bone</u>.'

READING PASSAGE 3

27	Y	PARAGRAPH 1 tells us that the first commercial fishermen cast their nets and hooks over a thousand years ago.
28	Y	PARAGRAPH 2 supports the statement by stating that, in general, we view the oceans as something which should be open to all.
29	N	PARAGRAPH 2 contradicts the statement when it says that '... most marine protected areas allow some fishing to continue.'
30	NG	The passage focuses on ways of protecting *supplies* of fish; it does not discuss the option of limiting *consumer demand*.
31	N	PARAGRAPH 4 makes it clear that destruction of the variety of mammals has been much easier than their recovery will be to manage.
32	D	The writer means that pleas from fisheries' managers for more time to make their models work, delay action which might lead to real success.
33	C	None of the statements A, B or D is supported by the passage, but in PARAGRAPH 5 the writer says: 'The Common Fisheries Policy exemplifies the worst pitfalls: flawed models ... .' Which agrees with statement C.
34	A	In PARAGRAPH 6 the writer says: 'We can go a long way to avoiding this catastrophic mistake with simple common-sense management ...' thus supporting statement A. Statements B, C and D are contradicted in the passage.

35	B	PARAGRAPH 1 *'by the nineteenth century it was still felt, justifiably, that the plentiful resources of the sea were … beyond the reach of fishing, and so <u>there was little need to restrict fishing or create protected areas.'</u>*
36	F	PARAGRAPH 1 *'… modern <u>fishing technologies</u> leave fish no place to hide …'*
37	D	PARAGRAPH 1 *'… the only refuges from fishing are those we deliberately create.'* PARAGRAPH 5 *'creating marine reserves … has been tried and refined for the last fifty years.'*
38	I	PARAGRAPH 1 *'… the sea trails far behind the <u>land</u> in terms of the area and the quality of protection given.'*
39	H	PARAGRAPH 5 *'To some people, creating <u>marine reserves</u> is an admission of failure.'*
40	C	PARAGRAPH 6 *'If we don't break out of this <u>cycle of failure</u>, humanity will lose a key source of protein, and much more besides. Disrupting natural ecosystem processes … could have ramifications for human life itself.'*

Test 7 WRITING

Task 1 Model answer

The pie charts indicate that there are some major differences but also a number of similarities in the proportion of time younger and older people spend on six different activities in the Internet.

The most noticeable difference relates to the most popular activity for each of the groups. Social networking is the most favoured activity for the younger group, accounting for 24 percent of their time on the Internet. This contrasts with just eight percent spent on this by 60 to 70 year olds. The largest percentage of Internet time for older users (29 percent) was spent on making bookings, for example for travel, while for younger users this was their least popular activity, at just five percent.

In other activities there were surprisingly similar percentages for the two groups. Both groups spent a fairly large amount of time researching, for example, health matters (26 percent for older people, 20 percent for younger). The younger age group spent 21 percent of their time accessing music and films but this was only four percent more than the older age group. Finally, there was only two percent difference between the two groups in the proportion of time they spent buying things on the Internet.

Task 2 Model answer

It is widely agreed that a happy and stable relationship in marriage is the bedrock of any community, with a greater likelihood of responsible partners, and if children result, harmonious families. Because of this, it is important to support the institution of marriage in every way possible. One important question in relation to this is: at what age should couples be allowed to marry?

There are a number of reasons for making the minimum legal age for matrimony as late as possible. Many would argue that people in their 20s are able to make much more rational and informed decisions than teenagers can. Older people will have seen enough of the world to know that that the feelings they hold for someone at a given moment may not last. They will realise that superficial characteristics like physical beauty or sporting prowess may not be the only ones to bring happiness in a relationship. Older couples are likely to give more consideration to issues such as income and job prospects, but also to less obvious but important personality traits such as tolerance, kindness or moral strength.

However, other people contend that it is unrealistic to make couples wait until their 20s before marrying. They suggest that as soon as the boy and girl have reached puberty they should be allowed to marry. To prevent them doing so would result in resentment between the generations, frustration and an increase in the number of unsupported pregnancies. If married teenagers are given enough help and support, they can have children when they are young and healthy enough to enjoy them.

Taking into account both these sets of arguments, I feel that 21 is probably too old but that 18 should be made the legal minimum at which couples can marry.

General training

Reading
SECTION 1

1	E	*'Pink, blue, green, silver or brown – please state preference.'*
2	B	*'this set is suitable for a broad range of sizes'*
3	E	*'This item is not available for overseas delivery'*
4	D	*'for all young children who want to copy adults and do some real woodworking.'*
5	A	*'A great product for keeping young children entertained in the bath.'* (implies the product is made to be used in water)
6	F	*'A great creative kit for making an adorable ballerina doll.'*
7	C	*'This small xylophone …'*
8	F	The letter tells us in PARAGRAPH 1 that the Campbell Hotel is *'one of Scotland's oldest family-run hotels.'*

9	T	PARAGRAPH 2 says 'We have reserved a twin room for you …' In the UK, a twin room means a room with two beds.
10	NG	The letter does not say whether prices will be reduced or not for guests who do not have breakfast.
11	T	PARAGRAPH 3 says 'We are currently offering a special rate for Sunday nights – £25 per person …' (as opposed to the £55 normal rate).
12	T	PARAGRAPH 4 of the letter informs guests that: 'Check-in is from 2 p.m. …'
13	NG	The letter does not indicate whether dinner in the Loch Restaurant must be pre-booked.
14	F	PARAGRAPH 6 of the letter says that: 'If cancelled up to 24 hours before the day of arrival no fee will be charged. If cancelled later … then the first night will be charged in full.'

SECTION 2

15	website	PARAGRAPH 2 'Check our website to learn about volunteer positions available in your area.'
16	officer	PARAGRAPH 3 'Contact the DNR officer who is designated for the project …'
17	schedule	PARAGRAPH 4 'Arrive on time (or a little early) to work on the project for which you registered to work. The schedule you agree to is important: be sure to call if you will be absent or need to leave early.'
18	public	PARAGRAPH 5 bullet point 1 'If working with the public in your volunteer position, all questions from them … are to be passed on to your supervisor.'
19	opinion	PARAGRAPH 5 bullet point 1 'Avoid expressing a personal opinion.'
20	hours	PARAGRAPH 5 bullet point 2 'Keep a note of your hours … turn in your records to your supervisor.'
21	needs	PARAGRAPH 5 bullet point 3 'Your supervisor will be happy to discuss any concerns that you may have, as well as any special needs …'

22	online networking	PARAGRAPH 4: '… online networking, using corporate sites such as LinkedIn, has also given employees the ability to liaise with people doing similar work …'
23	building trade	PARAGRAPH 5 '[For people who're working in digital media it's everything], but in the building trade it's almost pointless …'
24	formal courses	PARAGRAPH 7 'Apart from on-the-job training, there are self-help books … as well as formal courses.'
25	Staff Development	PARAGRAPH 7 '… decide what their genuine areas of weakness are, and then talk about them with their Staff Development coordinator …'
26	job shadowing	PARAGRAPH 8 '… temporary roles or job-shadowing can give you a more rounded view of the organisation.'
27	targets	PARAGRAPH 10 'One of the key skills is dealing with your boss, and part of that is knowing what your boss is being judged by. They all have targets …'

SECTION 3

28	iii	PARAGRAPH A describes the wide range of geographical areas in which the Spotted Flycatcher has been observed at different times of the year.
29	v	PARAGRAPH B outlines records kept in the eighteenth century of very regular patterns of the bird's arrival in England and compares this with modern records.
30	i	PARAGRAPH C shows how the female undertakes most of the nest building and incubation, but that the male ensures the eggs are kept warm while the female leaves the nest to feed.
31	viii	PARAGRAPH D does briefly refer to predators, but mainly describes the way the parent birds care for the chicks in the early days.
32	iv	PARAGRAPH E describes the way the birds change their insect-catching pattern according to changes in temperature.

33	ix	PARAGRAPH F outlines the appearance of the bird and other means of identification.
34	vii	PARAGRAPH G shows the work being carried out to gather and understand data on declining numbers as a first step towards conservation.
35	drab/dull	PARAGRAPH A: '*Despite its rather <u>dull</u> plumage*' PARAGRAPH F: '*The Spotted Flycatcher lacks the more brightly marked plumage of many other birds, and … it can be mistaken for another, equally <u>drab</u> species …*'
36	perch	PARAGRAPH F: '*… seldom seen on the ground, but usually feed from a <u>perch</u>, making sallies after aerial insects.*'
37	family	PARAGRAPH F: '*… it is rare to see several Spotted Flycatchers together unless they happen to be a <u>family</u> …*'
38	snapping sound	PARAGRAPH F '*the audible <u>snapping sound</u> that the bill sometimes makes when the bird snatches an insect from the air.*'
39	D	PARAGRAPH A tells us that the birds have been sighted in the northern hemisphere (Britain) and the southern hemisphere (Africa). (D). Statements A, B and C are contradicted in PARAGRAPHS A and B of the passage.
40	B	PARAGRAPH D confirms that the nest may be used for more than one brood (B). A cannot be chosen as PARAGRAPH C describes the nest as '*delicate*'. C and D are also contradicted in PARAGRAPH C.

General Training Writing

Task 1 Model answer

Dear Alice

I hope you're well and enjoying being back at university after the holiday.

I wonder if you could do me a favour. Would it be possible to buy some books suitable for a 14 year old boy? My friend (Jasmine) has a son who is not doing particularly well in his English classes at school. His English is actually quite good, but he's lost motivation and Jasmine wondered whether it might help if he could be persuaded to do some more reading in the language. As you know, it's very difficult to get hold of English books here and the ones in the bookshops are rather boring for a teenage boy.

As you have two younger brothers, I thought you might have some suggestions about what he would enjoy.

If you could choose a couple of books, Jasmine would be very happy to send money to cover the cost of the books and postage. I hope you don't mind my asking you to do this and do let me know if there's anything I can send you from here to say thank you.

Best wishes

Sasha

Task 2 Model answer

Unquestionably there are many more cars on the roads now than there were even ten years ago but whether there are <u>too</u> many, and they are ruining our urban areas, is a matter of some dispute.

The main arguments against this point of view are as follows. Firstly, we cannot claim that there are too many cars in a given place if the majority of people there feel the numbers are acceptable. Secondly, it is wrong to deprive people of the right to drive their own cars. Public transport is often so poor that it is not a realistic option. Only private cars can enable people to go about their daily lives efficiently and comfortably, for example, commuting to work and going shopping. Thirdly, in most urban areas, even the most congested ones, it is still possible to drive round fairly easily. Buses and bicycles often have special lanes so all forms of transport can co-exist happily together.

However, I feel strongly that there are too many cars in our towns and cities. Roads are becoming more dangerous, with many more serious road accidents occurring, affecting everyone, including those in cars. Pedestrians and cyclists have less and less space and freedom to move safely. Another point to consider is that large numbers of cars are causing severe pollution, making the air of our cities unpleasant; at times, almost unbreathable. There has been a sharp rise in the number of people suffering from respiratory diseases, and old and valued buildings are being destroyed by chemicals from car exhausts.

Thus, although many people fiercely defend the right of choice to drive cars in cities, I believe steps should be taken to reduce their number before they end up taking over and ruining our urban environments.